W9-CLP-231

Hac...
Major documents in
American economic
history

MAJOR DOCUMENTS IN AMERICAN ECONOMIC HISTORY

Vol. I: From an Agrarian to an Industrial Economy (1785-1900)

LOUIS M. HACKER

Professor of Economics
Columbia University

AN ANVIL ORIGINAL
under the general editorship of
LOUIS L. SNYDER

D. VAN NOSTRAND COMPANY, INC.
PRINCETON, NEW JERSEY
TORONTO   LONDON
NEW YORK

To
Helen
and
Phillip W. Haberman

D. VAN NOSTRAND COMPANY, INC.
120 Alexander St., Princeton, New Jersey (*Principal office*); 24 West 40 St., New York, N.Y.
D. VAN NOSTRAND COMPANY (Canada), LTD.
25 Hollinger Rd., Toronto 16, Canada
D. VAN NOSTRAND COMPANY, LTD.
358, Kensington High Street, London, W.14, England

COPYRIGHT © 1961, BY
LOUIS M. HACKER
Published simultaneously in Canada by
D. Van Nostrand Company (Canada), Ltd.

PREFACE

These volumes are a companion piece to my earlier *American Capitalism: Its Promise and Accomplishment,* which also appeared as an Anvil Original. In this first part, I have sought to trace—using in almost every case public documents—the problems of the United States as it moved from an agrarian to an industrial economy. I have focused my attention on the concerns and the actions of public authority; for I have wanted to show the impact of policy upon the development of the American people. As we were transformed—slowly up to about 1860; with great rapidity from the Civil War to 1900—and in due time became one of the great industrial nations of the earth, we had to come to grips with all those many questions that could aid or impede growth. Public authority, in consequence, concerned itself with the Land, Manufactures and Tariff, Labor and Immigration, Transportation, and Money and Banking; and all of these questions are exemplified here in the documents I have gathered together.

In many ways this is an unusual collection, for the documents here printed are frequently cited but they rarely are easily available to the general reader and student. I hope, therefore, that this collection will find many uses, not only as a supplement to classroom work but for the reader who is curious about the exact wording of many incidents and events in American history with which he is familiar but which he has never encountered in their original form.

Louis M. Hacker

TABLE OF CONTENTS

— 1 —

ECONOMIC PROVISIONS OF THE CONSTITUTION OF THE UNITED STATES

By 1785 it was clear that the Confederation had proved inadequate to its tasks; in fact, the American Revolution itself was in danger. The Congress' inability to devise a fiscal policy—pay the country's debts, raise a revenue, regulate commerce—and the threat of internal disorders, and indeed breakdown, following Shays' Rebellion led to the meeting of the Constitutional Convention in 1787. The Convention had no difficulty in creating a broad general scheme to assure the new central government's survival as far as monetary and fiscal powers were concerned; it gave the Congress authority to protect property rights by investing in it control over bankruptcies; and it severely limited the functions of the States as regards economic matters generally. The economic provisions of the Constitution are to be found in Article I, sections 8, 9, and 10, and in Article VI. The Sixteenth Amendment (the power to lay and collect income taxes) is also included here. The proposed Amendment was sent to the States on July 12, 1909, by the Sixty-first Congress; it became effective February 25, 1913.

✓   ✓   ✓

ARTICLE I

SECTION 8

GENERAL POWERS OF CONGRESS.

The Congress shall have Power.—1. To lay and collect Taxes, Duties, Imposts and Excises, to pay the Debts and

provide for the common Defence and general Welfare of
the United States; but all Duties, Imposts and Excises
shall be uniform throughout the United States;

Borrowing of money.—2. To borrow Money on the
credit of the United States;

Regulation of commerce.—3. To regulate Commerce
with foreign Nations, and among the several States, and
with the Indian Tribes;

Naturalization and bankruptcy.—4. To establish an uniform Rule of Naturalization, and uniform Laws on the
subject of Bankruptcies throughout the United States;

Money, weights and measures.—5. To coin Money, regulate the Value thereof, and of foreign Coin, and fix the
Standard of Weights and Measures;

Counterfeiting.—6. To provide for the Punishment of
counterfeiting the Securities and current Coin of the
United States;

Post offices.—7. To establish Post Offices and post
Roads;

Patents and copyrights.—8. To promote the Progress of
Science and useful Arts, by securing for limited Times to
Authors and Inventors the exclusive Right to their respec-
tive Writings and Discoveries;

To enact laws necessary to enforce Constitution.—18.
To make all Laws which shall be necessary and proper for
carrying into Execution the foregoing Powers, and all
other Powers vested by this Constitution in the Government of the United States, or in any Department or Officer
thereof.

SECTION 9

Capitation and other direct taxes.—4. No Capitation, or
other direct, Tax shall be laid, unless in Proportion to the
Census or Enumeration herein before directed to be taken.

Exports not to be taxed.—5. No Tax or Duty shall be
laid on Articles exported from any State.

*No preference to be given to ports of any State: inter-
state shipping.*—6. No Preference shall be given by any
Regulation of Commerce or Revenue to the Ports of one
State over those of another: nor shall Vessels bound to,
or from, one State, be obliged to enter, clear, or pay Duties
in another.

Money, how drawn from treasury; financial statements to be published.—7. No money shall be drawn from the Treasury, but in Consequence of Appropriations made by Law; and a regular Statement and Account of the Receipts and Expenditures of all public Money shall be published from time to time.

SECTION 10

Limitations of the powers of the several States.—1. No State shall enter into any Treaty, Alliance, or Confederation; grant Letters of Marque and Reprisal; coin Money; emit Bills of Credit; make any Thing but gold and silver Coin a Tender in Payment of Debts; pass any Bill of Attainder, ex post facto Law, or Law impairing the Obligation of Contracts, or grant any Title of Nobility.

State imposts and duties.—2. No State shall, without the Consent of the Congress, lay any Imposts or Duties on Imports or Exports, except what may be absolutely necessary for executing its inspection Laws: and the net Produce of all Duties and Imposts, laid by any State on Imports or Exports, shall be for the Use of the Treasury of the United States; and all such Laws shall be subject to the Revision and Control of the Congress.

Further restrictions on powers of States.—3. No State shall, without the Consent of Congress, lay any Duty of Tonnage, keep Troops, or Ships of War in time of Peace, enter into any Agreement or Compact with another State, or with a foreign Power, or engage in War, unless actually invaded, or in such imminent Danger as will not admit of delay.

ARTICLE VI

Debts contracted under the confederation secured.—1. All Debts contracted and Engagements entered into, before the Adoption of this Constitution, shall be as valid against the United States under this Constitution, as under the Confederation.

Constitution, laws and treaties of the United States to be supreme.—2. This Constitution, and the Laws of the United States which shall be made in Pursuance thereof; and all Treaties made, or which shall be made, under the Authority of the United States, shall be the supreme Law

of the Land; and the Judges in every State shall be bound
thereby, any Thing in the Constitution or Laws of any
State to the Contrary notwithstanding.

AMENDMENT XVI

(The proposed amendment was sent to the states July 12,
1909, by the Sixty-first Congress. It became effective Feb.
25, 1913.)

*Taxes on income; Congress given power to lay and col-
lect.*—The Congress shall have power to lay and collect
taxes on incomes, from whatever source derived, without
apportionment among the several States, and without regard to any census or enumeration.

— 2 —

THE LAND ORDINANCE OF MAY 20, 1785[1]

In order to obtain revenue—for the Confederation was hard pressed—the Continental Congress provided for the surveying and sale of the lands in the Northwest Territory. These lands were to be laid out in townships and in turn to be divided into sections each a mile square, or 640 acres. This became the classical pattern of land distribution in the United States.

LAND

Be it ordained by the United States in Congress assembled that the territory ceded by individual States to the United States, which has been purchased of the Indian inhabitants shall be disposed of in the following manner: . . . The Surveyors as they are respectively qualified shall proceed to divide the said territory into townships of six miles square, by lines running due north and south and others crossing those at right angles as near as may be, unless where the boundaries of the late Indian purchases may render the same impracticable, and then they shall depart from this rule no farther than such particular circumstances may require. . . . The plats of the townships respectively, shall be marked by subdivisions into lots of one mile square, or 640 acres, in the same direction as the external lines, and numbered from 1 to 36; always beginning the succeeding range of the lots with the number next to that with which the preceding one concluded. And

[1] *Journals of the Continental Congress,* Vol. 28, pp. 375-381.

where, from the causes before mentioned, only a fractional part of a township shall be surveyed, the lots, protracted thereon, shall bear the same numbers as if the township had been entire. And the surveyors, in running the external lines of the townships, shall, at the interval of every mile, mark corners for the lots which are adjacent, always designating the same in a different manner from those of the townships. . . .

As soon as seven ranges of townships, and fractional parts of townships, in the direction from south to north, shall have been surveyed, the geographer shall transmit plats thereof to the board of treasury, who shall record the same, with the report, in well bound books to be kept for that purpose. And the geographer shall make similar returns, from time to time, of every seven ranges as they may be surveyed. The Secretary at War shall have recourse thereto, and shall take by lot therefrom, a number of townships, and fractional parts of townships, as well from those to be sold entire as from those to be sold in lots, as will be equal to one seventh part of the whole of such seven ranges, as nearly as may be, for the use of the late continental army; and he shall make a similar draught, from time to time, until a sufficient quantity is drawn to satisfy the same, to be applied in manner hereinafter directed. The board of treasury shall, from time to time, cause the remaining numbers, as well as those to be sold entire, as those to be sold in lots, to be drawn for, in the name of the thirteen states respectively, according to the quotas in the last preceding requisition on all the states; provided, that in case more land than its proportion is allotted for sale, in any state, at any distribution, a deduction be made therefor at the next.

The board of treasury shall transmit a copy of the original plats, previously noting thereon, the townships, and fractional parts of townships, which shall have fallen to the several states, by the distribution aforesaid, to the Commissioners of the loan office of the several states, who, after giving notice of not less than two nor more than six months, by causing advertisements to be posted up at the court houses, or other noted places in every county, and to be inserted in one newspaper, published in the states of their residence respectively, shall proceed to sell the townships, or fractional parts of townships, at public vendue, in the following manner, viz: The township, or fractional part of a township, N 1, in the first range, shall be sold entire; and N 2, in the same range, by lots; and thus in alternate order through the whole of the first range. The township, or fractional part of a township, N 1, in the second range, shall be sold by lots; and N 2, in the same range, entire; and so in alternate order through the whole of the second range; and the third range shall be sold in the same manner as the first, and the fourth in the same manner as the second, and thus alternately throughout all the ranges; provided, that none of the lands, within the said territory, be sold under the price of one dollar the acre, to be paid in specie, or loan office certificates, reduced to specie value, by the scale of depreciation, or certificates of liquidated debts of the United States, including interest, besides the expense of the survey and other charges thereon, which are hereby rated at thirty six dollars the township, in specie, or certificates as aforesaid, and so in the same proportion for a fractional part of a township, or of a lot, to be paid at the time of sales; on failure of which payment, the said lands shall again be offered for sale.

There shall be reserved for the United States out of every township, the four lots, being numbered 8, 11, 26, 29, and out of every fractional part of a township, so many lots of the same numbers as shall be found thereon, for future sale. There shall be reserved the lot N 16, of every township, for the maintenance of public schools, within the said township; also one third part of all gold, silver, lead and copper mines, to be sold, or otherwise disposed of as Congress shall hereafter direct.

When any township, or fractional part of a township, shall have been sold as aforesaid, and the money or certificates received therefor, the loan officer shall deliver a deed in the following terms:

The United States of America, to all to whom these presents shall come, greeting:

Know ye, That for the consideration of   dollars, we have granted, and hereby do grant and confirm unto the township, (or fractional part of a township, as the case may be) numbered   in the range   excepting therefrom, and reserving one third part of all gold, silver, lead and copper mines within the same; and the lots Ns 8, 11, 26, and 29, for future sale or disposition, and the lot N 16, for the maintenance of public schools. To have to the said   his heirs and assigns for ever; (or if more than one purchaser, to the said   their heirs and assigns forever as tenants in Common.) In witness whereof, (A. B.) Commissioner of the loan office, in the State of   hath, in conformity to the Ordinance passed by the United States in Congress assembled, the twentieth day of May, in the year of our Lord one thousand seven hundred and eighty five, hereunto set his hand, and affixed his seal, this   day of   in the year of our Lord   and of the independence of the United States of America. . . .

THE TARIFF AND TONNAGE ACTS OF JULY 4, AND JULY 20, 1789 [2]

One of the great failures of the Confederation had been the Congress' inability to obtain unanimous approval from the States to raise a revenue, notably through import duties. No sooner was the new federal government, organized under the Constitution, installed than James Madison laid before the House of Representatives a measure for taxing imports. After seven weeks of debate a bill was passed—fixing specific duties on over 30 kinds of foreign goods, and ad valorem duties from 7½ to 15 per cent on a few specified articles. The average rate of duty, on an ad valorem basis, was about 8½ per cent.

Another measure had to do with imposing duties on tonnage whose purpose was to favor American ships and thus foster the building of a domestic merchant marine.

Undoubtedly a revenue was the first consideration of Congress; but the tariff act also included unmistakable protective features. Thus the United States was launched upon a career of tariff-making and tinkering until the passage of the Reciprocal Trade Agreements Act of 1934.

✦　　　✦　　　✦

An Act for laying a duty on goods, wares, and merchandises, imported into the United States.

Whereas it is necessary for the support of Government, for the discharge of the debts of the United States, and

[2] *Annals of Congress,* 1st Congress, 1st Session, Appendix, pp. 2183-2186.

the encouragement and protection of manufactures, that duties be laid on goods, wares, and merchandises, imported.

Be it enacted, &c. That from and after the first day of August next ensuing, the several duties hereinafter mentioned shall be laid on the following goods, wares, and merchandises, imported into the United States from any foreign port or place, that is to say—

On all distilled spirits of Jamaica proof, imported from any kingdom or country whatsoever, per gallon, ten cents;

On all other distilled spirits, per gallon, eight cents;

On molasses, per gallon, two and a half cents;

On Madeira wine, per gallon, eighteen cents;

On all other wines, per gallon, ten cents;

On every gallon of beer, ale, or porter, in casks, five cents;

On all cider, beer, ale, or porter, in bottles, per dozen, twenty cents.

On malt, per bushel, ten cents;

On brown sugars, per pound, one cent;

On loaf sugars, per pound, three cents;

On all other sugars, per pound, one and a half cents;

On coffee, per pound, two and a half cents;

On cocoa, per pound, one cent;

On all candles of tallow, per pound, two cents;

On all candles of wax or spermaceti, per pound, six cents;

On cheese, per pound, four cents;

On soap, per pound, two cents;

On boots, per pair, fifty cents;

On all shoes, slippers, or galoshoes, made of leather, per pair, seven cents;

On all shoes or slippers made of silk or stuff, per pair, ten cents;

On cables, for every one hundred and twelve pounds, seventy-five cents;

On tarred cordage, for every one hundred and twelve pounds, seventy-five cents;

On untarred cordage and yarn, for every one hundred and twelve pounds, ninety cents;

On twine or pack-thread, for every one hundred and twelve pounds, two hundred cents;

On all steel unwrought, for every one hundred and twelve pounds, fifty-six cents;

On all nails and spikes, per pound, one cent;

On salt, per bushel, six cents;

On manufactured tobacco, per pound, six cents;

On snuff, per pound, ten cents;

On indigo, per pound, sixteen cents;

On wool and cotton cards, per dozen, fifty cents;

On coal, per bushel, two cents;

On pickled fish, per barrel, seventy-five cents;

On dried fish, per quintal, fifty cents;

On all teas imported from China or India, in ships built in the United States, and belonging to a citizen or citizens thereof, or in ships or vessels built in foreign countries, and on the sixteenth day of May last wholly the property of a citizen or citizens of the United States, and so continuing until the time of importation, as follows:

On bohea tea, per pound, six cents;

On all souchong, or other black teas, per pound, ten cents;

On all hyson teas, per pound, twenty cents;

On all other green teas, per pound, twelve cents;

On all teas imported from Europe in ships or vessels built in the United States, and belonging wholly to a citizen or citizens thereof, or in ships or vessels built in foreign countries, and on the sixteenth day of May last, wholly the property of a citizen or citizens of the United States, and so continuing until the time of importation, as follows:

On bohea tea, per pound, eight cents;

On all souchong, and other black teas, per pound, thirteen cents;

On all hyson teas, per pound, twenty-six cents;

On all other green teas, per pound, sixteen cents;

On all teas imported in any other manner than as above mentioned, as follows:

On bohea tea, per pound, fifteen cents;

On all souchong, or other black teas, per pound, twenty-two cents;

On all hyson teas, per pound, forty-five cents;

On all other green teas, per pound, twenty-seven cents;

On all goods, wares, and merchandises, other than teas, imported from China or India, in ships not built in the

United States, and not wholly the property of a citizen or citizens thereof, nor in vessels built in foreign countries, and on the sixteenth day of May last wholly the property of a citizen or citizens of the United States, and so continuing until the time of importation, twelve and a half per centum ad valorem.

On all looking glasses, window and other glass, (except black quart bottles)

On all China, stone, and earthern ware,

On gunpowder,

On all paints ground in oil,

On shoe and knee buckles,

On gold and silver lace, and

On gold and silver leaf, ten per centum ad valorem;

On all blank books,

On all writing, printing, or wrapping paper, paper hangings and pasteboard,

On all cabinet wares,

On all buttons,

On all saddles,

On all gloves of leather,

On all hats of beaver, fur, wood, or mixture of either,

On all millinery ready made,

On all castings of iron, and upon slit and rolled iron,

On all leather tanned or tawed, and all manufactures of leather, except such as shall be otherwise rated,

On canes, walking sticks, and whips,

On clothing ready-made,

On all brushes,

On gold, silver, and plated ware, and on jewellery and paste work,

On anchors, and on all wrought tin and pewter ware, seven and a half per centum ad valorem;

On playing cards, per pack, ten cents;

On every coach, chariot, or other four wheeled carriage, and on every chaise, solo, or other two wheeled carriage, or parts thereof, fifteen per centum ad valorem.

On all other goods, wares, and merchandise, five per centum on the value thereof at the time and place of importation, except as follows: Saltpetre, tin in pigs, tin plates, lead, old pewter, brass, iron and brass wire, copper in plates, wool, cotton, dying woods and dying drugs, raw hides, beaver, and all other furs and deer skins.

SEC. 2. *And be it further enacted,* That from and after the first day of December, which shall be in the year one thousand seven hundred and ninety, there shall be laid a duty on every one hundred and twelve pounds weight of hemp, imported as aforesaid, of sixty cents; and on cotton per pound, three cents.

SEC. 3. *And be it further enacted,* That all the duties paid, or secured to be paid, upon any of the goods, wares, and merchandises, as aforesaid, except on distilled spirits, other than brandy and geneva, shall be returned or discharged upon such of the said goods, wares, or merchandises, as shall, within twelve months after payment made, or security given, be exported to any country without the limits of the United States, as settled by the late treaty of peace; except one per centum on the amount of the said duties, in consideration of the expense which shall have accrued by the entry and safe keeping thereof.

SEC. 4. *And be it further enacted,* That there shall be allowed and paid on every quintal of dried, and on every barrel of pickled, fish, of the fisheries of the United States, and on every barrel of salted provision of the United States, exported to any country without the limits thereof, in lieu of a drawback of the duties imposed on the importation of the salt employed and expended therein, viz:

On every quintal of dried fish, five cents;

On every barrel of pickled fish, five cents;

On every barrel of salted provision, five cents.

SEC. 5. *And be it further enacted,* That a discount of ten per cent, on all the duties imposed by this act, shall be allowed on such goods, wares, and merchandises, as shall be imported in vessels built in the United States, and which shall be wholly the property of a citizen or citizens thereof, or in vessels built in foreign countries, and on the sixteenth day of May last, wholly the property of a citizen or citizens of the United States, and so continuing until the time of importation.

SEC. 6. *And be it further enacted,* That this act shall continue and be in force until the first day of June, which shall be in the year of our Lord one thousand seven hundred and ninety-six, and from thence until the end of the next succeeding session of Congress, which shall be held thereafter, and no longer.

An Act imposing duties on tonnage.

Be it enacted, &c., That the following duties shall be, and are hereby, imposed on all ships or vessels entered into the United States, that is to say:

On all ships or vessels built within the said States, and belonging wholly to a citizen or citizens thereof; or not built within the said States, but on the twenty-ninth day of May, one thousand seven hundred and eighty-nine, belonging, and during the time such ships or vessels shall continue to belong wholly to a citizen or citizens thereof, at the rate of six cents per ton. On all ships or vessels hereafter built in the United States, belonging wholly, or in part, to subjects of foreign powers, at the rate of thirty cents per ton. On all other ships or vessels, at the rate of fifty cents per ton.

SEC. 2. *Provided always, and be it enacted,* That no ship or vessel built within the aforesaid States, and belonging to a citizen or citizens thereof, shall, whilst employed in the coasting trade, or in the fisheries, pay tonnage more than once in any year.

SEC. 3. *And be it further enacted,* That every ship or vessel employed in the transportation of any of the produce or manufactures of the United States, coastwise, within the said States, except such ship or vessel be built within the said States, and belong to a citizen or citizens thereof, shall, on each entry, pay fifty cents per ton.

SEC. 4. *And be it further enacted,* That this act shall commence and be in force from and after the fifteenth day of August next.

— 4 —

ESTABLISHING THE FIRST BANK OF THE UNITED STATES, FEBRUARY 25, 1791 [3]

Alexander Hamilton, in his efforts to put the new Republic on a sound basis, saw the necessity for the creation of a Bank which would protect the money supply of the country and perform important fiscal functions for the government. Over the opposition of Thomas Jefferson, he was able to persuade Congress (and President Washington) to set up such a Bank; this Congress did, chartering it for 20 years.

1   1   1

An Act to incorporate the subscribers to the Bank of the United States.

Whereas it is conceived that the establishment of a bank for the United States, upon a foundation sufficiently extensive to answer the purposes intended thereby, and at the same time upon the principles which afford adequate security for an upright and prudent administration thereof, will be very conducive to the successful conducting of the national finances; will tend to give facility to the obtaining of loans, for the use of the Government, in sudden emergencies, and will be productive of considerable advantage to trade and industry in general:

Therefore,

Be it enacted, &c., That a Bank of the United States shall be established; the capital stock whereof shall not

[3] *Annals of Congress,* 1st Congress, 3rd Session, Appendix, pp. 2375-2381.

21

exceed ten millions of dollars, divided into twenty-five thousand shares, each share being four hundred dollars . . .

SEC. 2. *And be it further enacted,* That it shall be lawful for any person, co-partnership, or body politic, to subscribe for such or so many shares as he, she, or they shall think fit, not exceeding one thousand, except as shall be hereafter directed relatively to the United States; and that the sums respectively subscribed, except on behalf of the United States, shall be payable one-fourth in gold and silver, and three-fourths in that part of the public debt, which, according to the loan proposed in the fourth and fifteenth sections of the act, entitled "An act making provision for the debt of the United States," shall bear an accruing interest, at the time of payment of six per centum per annum, and shall also be payable in four equal parts, in the aforesaid ratio of specie to debt, at the distance of six calendar months from each other; the first whereof shall be paid at time of subscription.

SEC. 3. *And be it further enacted,* That all those who shall become subscribers to the said bank, their successors and assigns shall be, and are hereby created and made a corporation and body politic, by the name and style of "The President, Directors, and Company of the Bank of the United States;" and shall so continue until the fourth of March, one thousand eight hundred and eleven: and by that name shall be, and are hereby, made able and capable in law, to have, purchase, receive, possess, enjoy, and retain to them and their successors, lands, rents, tenements, hereditaments, goods, chattels, and effects of what kind, nature, or quality soever, to an amount not exceeding in the whole fifteen millions of dollars, including the amount of the capital stock aforesaid . . .

SEC. 4. *And be it further enacted,* That for the well ordering of the affairs of the said corporation there shall be twenty-five directors; of whom there shall be an election on the first Monday of January in each year, by the stockholders or proprietors of the capital stock of the said corporation, and by plurality of the votes actually given; and those who shall be duly chosen at any election, shall be capable of serving as directors, by virtue of such choice, until the end or expiration of the Monday of January next ensuing the time of such election, and no longer. . . .

SEC. 7. *And be it further enacted,* That the following rules, restrictions, limitations, and provisions shall form and be fundamental articles of the Constitution of the said corporation, viz:

I. The number of votes to which each stockholder shall be entitled, shall be according to the number of shares he shall hold, in the proportions following: that is to say, for one share, and not more than two shares, one vote; for every two shares above two, and not exceeding ten, one vote; for every four shares above ten, and not exceeding thirty, one vote; for every six shares above thirty, and not exceeding sixty, one vote; for every eight shares above sixty, and not exceeding one hundred, one vote; and for every ten shares above one hundred, one vote; but no person, co-partnership, or body politic shall be entitled to a greater number than thirty votes. And after the first election, no share or shares shall confer a right of suffrage, which shall not have been holden three calendar months previous to the day of election. Stockholders actually resident within the United States, and none other, may vote in elections by proxy.

II. Not more than three-fourths of the directors in office, exclusive of the president, shall be eligible for the next succeeding year; but the director, who shall be president at the time of an election, may always be re-elected.

III. None but a stockholder, being a citizen of the United States, shall be eligible as a director. . . .

VIII. The lands, tenements, and hereditaments which it shall be lawful for the said corporation to hold, shall be only such as shall be requisite for its immediate accommodation in relation to the convenient transacting of its business, and such as shall have been *bonafide* mortgaged to it by way of security, or conveyed to it in satisfaction of debts previously contracted in the course of its dealings, or purchased at sales upon judgments which shall have been obtained for such debts.

IX. The total amount of the debts, which the said corporation shall at any time owe, whether by bond, bill, note, or other contract, shall not exceed the sum of ten millions of dollars, over and above the moneys then actually deposited in the bank for safe-keeping, unless the contracting of any greater debt shall have been previously authorized by a law of the United States. . . .

X. The said corporations may sell any part of the public debt whereof its stock shall be composed, but shall not be at liberty to purchase any public debt whatsoever; nor shall directly or indirectly deal or trade in any thing, except bills of exchange, gold or silver bullion, or in the sale of goods really and truly pledged for money lent and not redeemed in due time; or of goods which shall be the produce of its lands. Neither shall the said corporation take more than at the rate of six per centum per annum, for or upon its loans or discounts.

XI. No loan shall be made by the said corporation, for the use or on account of the Government of the United States, to an amount exceeding one hundred thousand dollars, or of any particular State, to an amount exceeding fifty thousand dollars, or of any foreign prince or State, unless previously authorized by a law of the United States. . . .

XIII. The bills obligatory and of credit, under the seal of the said corporation, which shall be made to any person or persons, shall be assignable by endorsement thereupon, under the hand or hands of such person or persons, and of his, her, or their assignee or assignees, and so as absolutely to transfer and vest the property thereof in each and every assignee or assignees successively, and to enable such assignee or assignees to bring and maintain an action thereupon in his, her, or their own name or names. . . .

XIV. Half-yearly dividends shall be made of so much of the profits of the bank as shall appear to the directors advisable; and once in every three years the directors shall lay before the stockholders, at a general meeting, for their information, an exact and particular statement of the debts which shall have remained unpaid after the expiration of the original credit, for a period of treble the term of that credit; and of the surplus of profit, if any, after deducting losses and dividends. . . .

XV. It shall be lawful for the directors aforesaid, to establish offices wheresoever they shall think fit within the United States, for the purposes of discount and deposite only, and upon the same terms, and in the same manner, as shall be practised at the bank; and to commit the management of the said offices, and the making of the said discounts, to such persons, under such agreements, and subject to such regulations as they shall deem proper; not being contrary to law, or to the constitution of the bank.

XVI. The officer at the head of the Treasury Department of the United States shall be furnished, from time to time, as often as he may require, not exceeding once a week, with statements of the amount of the capital stock of the said corporation, and of the debts due to the same; of the moneys deposited therein; of the notes in circulation, and of the cash in hand; and shall have a right to inspect such general accounts in the books of the bank as shall relate to the said statements. *Provided,* That this shall not be construed to imply a right of inspecting the account of any private individual or individuals with the bank. . . .

SEC. 10. *And be it further enacted,* That the bills or notes of the said corporation, originally made payable, or which shall have become payable on demand, in gold and silver coin, shall be receivable in all payments to the United States.

SEC. 11. *And be it further enacted,* That it shall be lawful for the President of the United States, at any time or times, within eighteen months after the first day of April next, to cause a subscription to be made to the stock of the said corporation, as part of the aforesaid capital stock of ten millions of dollars, on behalf of the United States, to an amount not exceeding two millions of dollars, to be paid out of the moneys which shall be borrowed by virtue of either of the acts, the one entitled "An act making provision for the debt of the United States;" and the other entitled "An act making provision for the reduction of the public debt;" borrowing of the bank an equal sum, to be applied to the purposes for which the said moneys shall have been procured, reimbursable in ten years by equal annual instalments; or at any time sooner, or in any greater proportions that the Government may think fit.

SEC. 12. *And be it further enacted,* That no other bank shall be established by any future law of the United States, during the continuance of the corporation hereby created; for which the faith of the United States is hereby pledged.

— 5 —

HAMILTON ON THE SUBJECT OF MANUFACTURES, DECEMBER, 1791 [4]

In December, 1791, Alexander Hamilton presented another of his famous memoranda to Congress, this one having to do with the desirability of fostering manufactures in the United States. Leaning heavily on Adam Smith, he coupled—a very wise understanding of the processes of growth and development—industrialization with improvement in the nation's wealth and income. Toward this end "infant manufacture" needed government assistance through high duties and other devices, notably bounties. But Congress turned a deaf ear and it was not until 1861, in the midst of Civil War, that the Republican party launched the United States upon a continuing program of protectionism.

✦   ✦   ✦

. . . II. But, without contending for the superior productiveness of manufacturing industry, it may conduce to a better judgment of the policy which ought to be pursued respecting its encouragement, to contemplate the subject under some additional aspects, tending not only to confirm the idea that this kind of industry has been improperly represented as unproductive in itself, but to evince, in addition, that the establishment and diffusion of manufactures have the effect of rendering the total mass of useful and productive labor, in a community, greater than it would otherwise be. . . .

[4] *Works of Alexander Hamilton* (New York, 1910).

. . . Whether the value of the produce of the labor of the farmer be somewhat more or less than that of the artificer, is not material to the main scope of the argument, which, hitherto, has only aimed at showing that the one, as well as the other, occasions a positive augmentation of the total produce and revenue of the society.

It is now proper to proceed a step further, and to enumerate the principal circumstances from which it may be inferred that manufacturing establishments not only occasion a positive augmentation of the produce and revenue of the society, but that they contribute essentially to rendering them greater than they could possibly be without such establishments. These circumstances are:

1. The division of labor.
2. An extension of the use of machinery.
3. Additional employment to classes of the community not ordinarily engaged in the business.
4. The promoting of emigration from foreign countries.
5. The furnishing greater scope for the diversity of talents and dispositions, which discriminate men from each other.
6. The affording a more ample and various field for enterprise.
7. The creating, in some instances, a new, and securing, in all, a more certain and steady demand for the surplus produce of the soil.

Each of these circumstances has a considerable influence upon the total mass of industrious effort in a community; together, they add to it a degree of energy and effect which is not easily conceived. . . .

1. *As to the division of labor* . . . the mere separation of the occupation of the cultivator from that of the artificer, has the effect of augmenting the productive powers of labor, and with them, the total mass of the produce or revenue of a country. . . .

2. *As to an extension of the use of machinery* . . . It is an artificial force brought in aid of the natural force of man; and, to all the purposes of labor, is an increase of hands, an accession of strength, unencumbered too by the expense of maintaining the laborer. . . .

4. *As to the promoting of emigration from foreign countries* . . . Manufacturers who, listening to the power-

ful invitations of a better price for their fabrics or their labor, of greater cheapness of provisions and raw materials, of an exemption from the chief part of the taxes, burthens, and restraints which they endure in the Old World, of greater personal independence and consequence, under the operation of a more equal government, and of what is far more precious than mere religious toleration, a perfect equality of religious privileges, would probably flock from Europe to the United States, to pursue their own trades or professions, if they were once made sensible of the advantages they would enjoy. . . .

6. *As to the affording a more ample and various field for enterprise.* This also is of greater consequence in the general scale of national exertion than might, perhaps, on a superficial view be supposed, and has effects not altogether dissimilar from those of the circumstance last noticed (i.e., opening a wider scope to diversity of talents and temperament). To cherish and stimulate the activity of the human mind, by multiplying the objects of enterprise, is not among the least considerable of the expedients by which the wealth of a nation may be promoted. . . .

The spirit of enterprise, useful and prolific as it is, must necessarily be contracted or expanded, in proportion to the simplicity or variety of the occupations and productions which are to be found in a society. It must be less in a nation of mere cultivators, than in a nation of cultivators and merchants; less in a nation of cultivators and merchants, than in a nation of cultivators, artificers, and merchants.

7. *As to the creating, in some instances, a new, and securing in all, a more certain and steady demand* . . . It is evident that the exertions of the husbandman will be steady or fluctuating, vigorous or feeble, in proportion to the steadiness or fluctuation, adequateness or inadequateness, of the markets on which he must depend for the vent of the surplus which may be produced by his labor; and that such surplus, in the ordinary course of things, will be greater or less in the same proportion.

For the purpose of this vent, a domestic market is greatly to be preferred to a foreign one; because it is, in the nature of things, far more to be relied upon.

It is a primary object of the policy of nations, to be able to supply themselves with subsistence from their own soils; and manufacturing nations, as far as circumstances permit, endeavor to procure from the same source the raw materials necessary for their own fabrics. This disposition, urged by the spirit of monopoly, is sometimes even carried to an injudicious extreme . . . the effect of which is, that the manufacturing nations abridge the natural advantages of their situation, through an unwillingness to permit the agricultural countries to enjoy the advantages of theirs, and sacrifice the interests of a mutually beneficial intercourse to the vain project of selling every thing and buying nothing.

But it is also a consequence of the policy which has been noted, that the foreign demand for the produces of agricultural countries is, in a great degree rather casual and occasional, than certain or constant. . . .

Considering how fast and how much the progress of new settlements in the United States must increase the surplus produce of the soil, and weighing seriously the tendency of the system which prevails among most of the commercial nations of Europe, whatever dependence may be placed on the force of natural circumstances to counteract the effects of an artificial policy, there appear strong reasons to regard the foreign demand for that surplus as too uncertain a reliance, and to desire a substitute for it in an extensive domestic market.

To secure such a market there is no other expedient than to promote manufacturing establishments. . . .

It merits particular observation, that the multiplication of manufactories not only furnishes a market for those articles which have been accustomed to be produced in abundance in a country, but it likewise creates a demand for such as were either unknown or produced in inconsiderable quantities. The bowels as well as the surface of the earth are ransacked for articles which were before neglected. Animals, plants, and minerals acquire a utility and a value which were before unexplored.

The foregoing considerations seem sufficient to establish, as general propositions, that it is the interest of nations to diversify the industrious pursuits of the individuals who compose them; that the establishment of manufactures is calculated not only to increase the general stock of useful and productive labor, but even to improve the state of agriculture in particular. . . .

— 6 —

THE WEALTH OF THE UNITED STATES AND FOREIGN INVESTMENTS IN IT, 1803 [5]

Thanks to the imagination and skill of Alexander Hamilton, as Secretary of the Treasury, the credit of the young Republic was securely established so that capital formation could take place as a result of domestic savings and investment, and notably the investments of foreigners in public issues and private enterprise. An early estimate of America's wealth was made by Samuel Blodget for 1805; he put this at $2.5 billion. (A 1958 estimate put the figure at $1,448 billion.) Blodget's detailed breakdown of foreign investments showed that a little less than half of American securities (in federal bonds, the stock of the Bank of the United States, and the stocks of state banks and state-chartered insurance companies and turnpike and canal companies) was foreign-owned. The new American nation could not have got off to its excellent start without this extraordinary flow of credit from abroad. Even the Louisiana Purchase was made possible only by English purchase of the bonds Jefferson floated to pay Napoleon.

✓   ✓   ✓

An Estimate of All the Real and Personal Property
in the United States

1 million of habitations and apparel for 6 millions of persons with shops, barns, implements,
tools, furniture, etc., each 360 dol. .... $ 360,000,000

[5] Samuel Blodget, *Economica: A Statistical Manual for the United States of America* (1806), pp. 196-198.

39 million acres of land averaged at 6 dol.	234,000,000
150 do. acres adjoining and near the cultivated lands averaged at 3½ dol.	525,000,000
451 million acres, the residue of all the lands in the U. S., averaged at 2 dol.	902,000,000
The carriages, horses, horned cattle, sheep, hogs, poultry and other live stock at 70 dol. each family	70,000,000
Turnpike, canal and toll bridge stock	15,000,000
10,000 flour, grist, saw, iron and other mills, value not less than 400 dol. each	4,000,000
1 million of slaves, averaged value 200 dolls. ..	200,000,000
Country produce on hand for exportation, manufacture, etc.	26,000,000
Stock in trade, viz. 1,000,000 tons shipping. European, India, merchandise, etc. in specie, bank stock, insurance stock and all other incorporated funds	150,000,000
Public buildings, churches, Washington city, lights, arsenals, naval and military stores, arms, ammunition, frigates, docks, yards, timber, etc., etc.	19,500,000
Total value for 1805	$2,505,500,000

FOREIGN INVESTMENTS AND TOTAL INVESTMENTS, JUNE 30, 1803

	FOREIGNERS				States	Incorporated Bodies	Domestic Individuals	Total Dollars
	English	Dutch	All Other Peoples	Total Foreign				
Total United States Securities	$15,882,797	$13,693,918	$2,542,495	$32,119,211	$5,608,564	$10,096,398	$22,330,606	$70,154,781
Louisiana 6s	9,250,000	1,500,000	500,000	11,250,000	—	—	—	11,250,000
Bank of the United States	4,000,000	2,000,000	200,000	6,200,000	—	120,000	3,680,000	10,000,000
Insurance Companies	500,000	—	—	500,000	100,000	400,000	8,000,000	9,000,000
State Banks	5,000,000	3,000,000	1,000,000	9,000,000	3,000,000	4,000,000	120,000	26,000,000
Turnpikes and Canals	100,000	80,000	—	180,000	—	100,000	3,120,000	3,400,000
Total	$34,732,797	$20,273,918	$4,242,495	$59,249,211	$8,708,564	$14,716,391	$36,010,606	$129,804,781

7

GALLATIN'S REPORT ON ROADS AND CANALS, APRIL 4, 1808[6]

At the request of the Senate, in 1807, the Secretary of the Treasury Albert Gallatin drew up a comprehensive report on the need for internal improvements, pointing to large-scale federal participation. The matter was one of continuing interest to Congress, and road-construction in particular once more began to receive attention and federal financing in the 1920's and in the 1950's.

THE SECRETARY OF THE TREASURY, in obedience to the resolution of the Senate of the 2d March, 1807, respectfully submits the following report on roads and canals. . . .

There are, however, some circumstances, which, whilst they render the facility of communications throughout the United States an object of primary importance, naturally check the application of private capital and enterprise to improvements on a large scale.

The price of labor is not considered as a formidable obstacle, because whatever it may be, it equally affects the expense of transportation, which is saved by the improvement, and that of effecting the improvement itself. The want of practical knowledge is no longer felt; and the occasional influence of mistaken local interests, in sometimes thwarting or giving an improper direction to public improvements, arises from the nature of man, and is common to all countries. The great demand for capital in the United States, and the extent of territory compared with the population, are, it is believed, the true causes which prevent

[6] *American State Papers,* Miscellaneous, Vol. 1 (1834).

new undertakings, and render those already accomplished less profitable than had been expected.

1. Notwithstanding the great increase of capital during the last fifteen years, the objects for which it is required continue to be more numerous, and its application is generally more profitable than in Europe. A small portion therefore is applied to objects which offer only the prospect of remote and moderate profit. And it also happens that a less sum being subscribed at first than is actually requisite for completing the work, this proceeds slowly; the capital applied remains unproductive for a much longer time than was necessary, and the interest accruing during that period becomes, in fact, an injurious addition to the real expense of the undertaking.

2. The present population of the United States, compared with the extent of territory over which it is spread, does not, except in the vicinity of the seaports, admit that extensive commercial intercourse within short distances, which, in England and some other countries, forms the principal support of artificial roads and canals. With a few exceptions, canals particularly cannot, in America, be undertaken with a view solely to the intercourse between the two extremes of, and along the intermediate ground which they occupy. It is necessary, in order to be productive, that the canal should open a communication with a natural extensive navigation which will flow though that new channel. It follows that whenever that navigation requires to be improved, or when it might at some distance be connected by another canal to another navigation, the first canal will remain comparatively unproductive until the other improvements are effected, until the other canal is also completed. Thus the intended canal between the Chesapeake and Delaware, will be deprived of the additional benefit arising from the intercourse between New York and the Chesapeake, until an inland navigation shall have been opened between the Delaware and New York. Thus the expensive canals completed around the falls of Potomac will become more and more productive in proportion to the improvement, first, of the navigation of the upper branches of the river, and then of its communication with the Western waters. Some works already executed are unprofitable; many more remain unattempted, because

their ultimate productiveness depends on other improvements, too extensive or too distant to be embraced by the same individuals.

The General Government can alone remove these obstacles.

With resources amply sufficient for the completion of every practicable improvement, it will always supply the capital wanted for any work which it may undertake, as fast as the work itself can progress; avoiding thereby the ruinous loss of interest on a dormant capital, and reducing the real expense to its lowest rate.

With these resources, and embracing the whole Union, it will complete on any given line all the improvements, however distant, which may be necessary to render the whole productive, and eminently beneficial.

The early and efficient aid of the *Federal* Government is recommended by still more important considerations. The inconveniences, complaints, and perhaps dangers, which may result from a vast extent of territory, can no otherwise be radically removed or prevented than by opening speedy and easy communications through all its parts. Good roads and canals will shorten distances, facilitate commercial and personal intercourse, and unite, by a still more intimate community of interests, the most remote quarters of the United States. No other single operation, within the power of Government, can more effectually tend to strengthen and perpetuate that Union which secures external independence, domestic peace, and internal liberty. . . .

The improvements which have been respectfully suggested as most important in order to facilitate the communication between the great geographical divisions of the United States will now be recapitulated.

I. From north to south, in a direction
    parallel to the seacoast.
    1. Canals opening an inland navigation for sea vessels from Massachusetts to North Carolina, being more than two-thirds of the Atlantic seacoast of the United States, and across all the principal capes, Cape Fear excepted, ... $3,000,000

2. A great turnpike road from Maine
to Georgia along the whole extent
of the Atlantic seacoast, ... 4,800,000
——————— $7,800,000

II. From east to west, forming communications across the mountains between the Atlantic and western
rivers.
1. Improvement of the navigation of
four great Atlantic rivers, including
canals parallel to them, ... 1,500,000
2. Four firstrate turnpike roads from
those rivers across the mountains,
to the four corresponding western
rivers, ... 2,800,000
3. Canal around the falls of the Ohio, 300,000
4. Improvement of roads to Detroit,
St. Louis and New Orleans, . . 200,000
——————— 4,800,000

III. In a northern and northwestwardly
direction, forming inland navigations
between the Atlantic seacoast, and
the great lakes and the St. Lawrence.
1. Inland navigation between the North
river and Lake Champlain, . . . 800,000
2. Great inland navigation opened the
whole way by canals from the North
river to Lake Ontario, ... 2,200,000
3. Canal around the falls and rapids of
Niagara, opening a sloop navigation
from Lake Ontario to the upper lakes
as far as the extremities of Lake
Michigan, ... 1,000,000
——————— 4,000,000
Making, together, ... $16,600,000

IV. The great geographical features of the country have
been solely adhered to in pointing out those lines of communication; and these appear to embrace all the great interests of
the Union, and to be calculated to diffuse and increase the
national wealth in a very general way, by opening an intercourse between the remotest extremes of the United States.
Yet it must necessarily result from an adherence to that principle, that those parts of the Atlantic States through which the
great western and northwest communications will be carried,
must, in addition to the general advantages in which they will
participate, receive from those communications greater local

and immediate benefits than the Eastern and perhaps Southern States. As the expense must be defrayed from the general funds of the Union, justice, and, perhaps, policy not less than justice, seems to require that a number of local improvements, sufficient to equalize the advantages, should also be undertaken in those States, parts of States, or districts which are less immediately interested in those inland communications. Arithmetical precision cannot, indeed, be attained in objects of that kind; nor would an apportionment of the moneys applied according to the population of each State be either just or practicable, since roads and particularly canals are often of greater utility to the States which they unite, than to those through which they pass. But a sufficient number of local improvements, consisting either of roads or canals may, without any material difficulty, be selected, so as to do substantial justice and give general satisfaction. Without pretending to suggest what would be the additional sum necessary for that object, it will, for the sake of round numbers, be estimated at $3,400,000

Which, added to the sum estimated for general
    improvements, ...   16,600,000
Would make an aggregate of $20,000,000

Amongst the resources of the Union, there is one which, from its nature, seems more particularly applicable to internal improvements. Exclusively of Louisiana, the General Government possesses, in trust for the people of the United States, about one hundred millions of acres fit for cultivation, north of the river Ohio, and near fifty millions south of the State of Tennessee. For the disposition of these lands a plan has been adopted, calculated to enable every industrious citizen to become a freeholder, to secure indisputable titles to the purchasers, to obtain a national revenue, and, above all, to suppress monopoly. Its success has surpassed that of every former attempt, and exceeded the expectations of its authors. But a higher price than had usually been paid for waste lands by the first inhabitants of the frontier became an unavoidable ingredient of a system intended for general benefit, and was necessary, in order to prevent the public lands being engrossed by individuals possessing greater wealth, activity, and local advantages. It is believed that nothing could be more gratifying to the purchasers, and to the inhabitants of the Western States generally, or better calculated to remove popular objections, and to defeat insidious efforts, than the application of the proceeds of the sales to improvements conferring general advantages on the nation, and an immediate benefit on the purchasers and inhabitants themselves. It may be added, that the United States, considered merely as owners of the soil, are also deeply interested in the opening of those communications which must necessarily enhance the value of their property. Thus the opening an inland navigation from tide water to the great lakes, would immediately give to the great body of lands bordering on those lakes as great value as if they were situated at the distance of one hundred miles by land from the seacoast. And if the proceeds of the first ten millions of acres which may be sold were applied to such improvements, the United States would be amply repaid in the sale of the other ninety millions. . . .

8

ESTABLISHING THE SECOND BANK OF THE UNITED STATES, APRIL 10, 1816[7]

The First Bank was permitted to lapse in 1811 as a result of the hostility of Jefferson and his friends. But it was too important an institution—as a regulator of the currency, as a fiscal agency of the Treasury—for the country to do without it; the result was the authorization of the Second Bank in 1816, also for 20 years. But an effort to renew the Bank's charter failed in 1832, when President Andrew Jackson vetoed the bill; and thus, in 1836, ended central banking in the United States until 1914, when the Federal Reserve System was established.

✓   ✓   ✓

SEC. 3. *And be it further enacted,* That it shall be lawful for any individual, company, corporation, or State, when the subscriptions shall be opened as hereinbefore directed, to subscribe for any number of shares of the capital of the said bank, not exceeding three thousand shares, and the sums so subscribed shall be payable, and paid, in the manner following: that is to say, seven millions of dollars thereof in gold or silver coin of the United States, or in gold coin of Spain, or the dominions of Spain, at the rate of one hundred cents for every twenty-eight grains and sixty hundredths of a grain of the actual weight thereof, or in other foreign gold or silver coin at the several rates prescribed by the first section of an act regulat-

---

[7] *Annals of Congress,* 14th Congress, 1st Session, pp. 1812-1822.

ing the currency of foreign coins in the United States, passed tenth day of April, one thousand eight hundred and six, and twenty-one millions of dollars thereof in like gold or silver coin, or in the funded debt of the United States contracted at the time of the subscriptions respectively. . . .

SEC. 6. *And be it further enacted,* That, at the opening of subscription to the capital stock of the said bank, the Secretary of the Treasury shall subscribe, or cause to be subscribed, on behalf of the United States, the said number of seventy thousand shares, amounting to seven millions of dollars as aforesaid, to be paid in gold or silver coin, or in stock of the United States, bearing interest at the rate of five per centum per annum; and if payment thereof or of any part thereof, be made in public stock, bearing interest as aforesaid, the said interest shall be payable quarterly, to commence from the time of making such payment on account of the said subscription, and the principal of the said stock shall be redeemable in any sums, and at any periods, which the Government shall deem fit. And the Secretary of the Treasury shall cause the certificates of such public stock to be prepared, and made in the usual form, and shall pay and deliver the same to the president, directors, and company, of the said bank on the first day of January, one thousand eight hundred and seventeen, which said stock it shall be lawful for the said president, directors, and company, to sell and transfer for gold and silver coin or bullion at their discretion: *Provided,* They shall not sell more than two millions of dollars thereof in any one year.

SEC. 7. *And be it further enacted,* That the subscribers to the said Bank of the United States of America, their successors and assigns, shall be, and are hereby, created a corporation and body politic, by the name and style of "The president, directors, and company, of the Bank of the United States," and shall so continue until the third day of March, in the year one thousand eight hundred and thirty-six, and by that name shall be, and are hereby, made able and capable, in law, to have, purchase, receive, possess, enjoy, and retain, to them and their successors, lands, rents, tenements, hereditaments, goods, chattels, and effects, of whatsover kind, nature, and quality, to an amount not exceeding, in the whole, fifty-five millions of dollars, including the amount of the capital stock aforesaid; and the same to sell, grant, demise, alien or dispose of . . .

SEC. 8. *And be it further enacted,* That, for the management of the affairs of the said corporation, there shall be twenty-five directors, five of whom, being stockholders, shall be annually appointed by the President of the United States, by and with the advice and consent of the Senate, not more than three of whom shall be residents of any one State; and twenty of whom shall be annually elected at the banking-house in the city of Philadelphia, on the first Monday of January, in each year, by the qualified stockholders of the capital of the said bank other than the United States, and by a plurality of votes then and there actually given, according to the scale of voting hereinafter prescribed . . .

SEC. 11. *And be it further enacted,* That the following rules, restrictions, limitations, and provisions, shall form and be fundamental articles of the constitution of the said corporation, to wit:

1. The number of votes to which the stockholders shall be entitled, in voting for directors, shall be according to the number of shares he, she, or they, respectively, shall hold, in the proportions following, that is to say, for one share and not more than two shares, one vote; for every two shares above two, and not exceeding ten, one vote; for every four shares above ten, and not exceeding thirty, one vote; for every six shares above thirty, and not exceeding sixty, one vote; for every eight shares above sixty, and not exceeding one hundred, one vote; and for every ten shares above one hundred, one vote; but no person, copartnership, or body politic, shall be entitled to a greater number than thirty votes; and after the first election, no share or shares shall confer a right of voting, which shall not have been holden three calendar months previous to the day of election. And stockholders actually resident within the United States, and none other, may vote in elections by proxy. . . .

3. None but a stockholder, resident citizen of the United States, shall be a director; nor shall a director be entitled to any emolument; but the directors may make such compensation to the president, for his extraordinary attendance at the bank, as shall appear to them reasonable. . . .

7. The lands, tenements, and hereditaments, which it

shall be lawful for the said corporation to hold, shall be only such as shall be requisite for its immediate accommodation in relation to the convenient transacting of its business, and such as shall have been *bona fide* mortgaged to it by way of security, or conveyed to it in satisfaction of debts previously contracted in the course of its dealings, or purchased at sales, upon judgments which shall have been obtained for such debts.

8. The total amount of debts which the said corporation shall at any time owe, whether by bond, bill, note, or other contract, over and above the debt or debts due for money deposited in the bank, shall not exceed the sum of thirty-five millions of dollars, unless the contracting of any greater debt shall have been previously authorized by law of the United States. . . .

9. The said corporation shall not, directly or indirectly, deal or trade in anything except bills of exchange, gold or silver bullion, or in the sale of goods really and truly pledged for money lent and not redeemed in due time, or goods which shall be the proceeds of its lands. It shall not be at liberty to purchase any public debt whatsoever, nor shall it take more than at the rate of six per centum per annum for or upon its loans or discounts.

10. No loan shall be made by the said corporation, for the use or on account of the Government of the United States, to an amount exceeding five hundred thousand dollars, or of any particular State, to an amount exceeding fifty thousand dollars, or of any foreign Prince or State, unless previously authorized by a law of the United States.

11. The stock of the said corporation shall be assignable and transferable, according to such rules as shall be instituted in that behalf, by the laws and ordinances of the same. . . .

13. Half-yearly dividends shall be made of so much of the profits of the bank as shall appear to the directors advisable; and once in every three years the directors shall lay before the stockholders, at a general meeting, for their information, an exact and particular statement of the debts which shall have remained unpaid after the expiration of the original credit, for a period of treble the term of that credit; and of the surplus of the profits, if any, after deducting losses and dividends. . . .

14. The directors of the said corporation shall establish a competent office of discount and deposite in the District of Columbia, whenever any law of the United States shall require such an establishment; also one such office of discount and deposite in any State in which two thousand shares shall have been subscribed or may be held, whenever, upon application of the Legislature of such State, Congress may, by law, require the same . . . And it shall be lawful for the directors of the said corporation to establish offices of discount and deposite, wheresoever they shall think fit, within the United States or the Territories thereof, and to commit the management of the said offices, and the business thereof, respectively, to such persons, and under such regulations, as the shall deem proper, not being contrary to law or the constitution of the bank. Or, instead of establishing such offices, it shall be lawful for the directors of the said corporation, from time to time, to employ any other bank or banks, to be first approved by the Secretary of the Treasury, at any place or places that they may deem safe and proper, to manage and transact the business proposed as aforesaid, other than for the purposes of discount, to be managed and transacted by such offices, under such agreements, and subject to such regulations, as they shall deem just and proper. Not more than thirteen, nor less than seven managers or directors, of every office established as aforesaid, shall be annually appointed by the directors of the bank, to serve one year; they shall choose a president from their own number; each of them shall be a citizen of the United States, and a resident of the State, Territory, or district, wherein such office is established; and not more than three-fourths of the said managers or directors, in office at the time of an annual appointment, shall be reappointed for the next succeeding year; and no director shall hold his office more than three years out of four, in succession; but the president may be always reappointed. . . .

16. No stockholder, unless he be a citizen of the United States, shall vote in the choice of directors.

17. No note shall be issued of less amount than five dollars. . . .

SEC. 14. *And be it further enacted,* That the bills or notes of the said corporation originally made payable, or which shall have become payable on demand, shall be receivable in all payments to the United States, unless otherwise directed by act of Congress.

SEC. 15. *And be it further enacted,* That during the continuance of this act, and whenever required by the Secretary of the Treasury, the said corporation shall give the necessary facilities for transferring the public funds from place to place, within the United States, or the Territories thereof, and for distributing the same in payment of the public creditors, without charging commissions or claiming allowance on account of difference in exchange, and shall also do and perform the several and respective duties of the Commissioners of Loans for the several States, or of any one or more of them, whenever required by law.

SEC. 16. *And be it further enacted,* That the deposites of the money of the United States, in places in which the said bank and branches thereof may be established, shall be made in said bank or branches thereof, unless the Secretary of the Treasury shall at any time otherwise order . . .

— 9 —

THE LAND LAW OF APRIL 24, 1820[8]

In 1820, Congress radically changed the basis of land distribution and sale, eliminating the credit system and providing for cash sales at $1.25 an acre in as little as half-quarter sections (80 acres).

✓   ✓   ✓

Be it enacted by the Senate and House of Representatives of the United States of America, in Congress assembled, That from and after the first day of July next, all the public lands of the United States, the sale of which is, or may be authorized by law, shall, when offered at public sale, to the highest bidder, be offered in half quarter sections; and when offered at private sale, may be purchased, at the option of the purchaser, either in entire sections, half sections, quarter sections, or half quarter sections . . .

SEC. 2. *And be it further enacted,* That credit shall not be allowed for the purchase money on the sale of any of the public lands which shall be sold after the first day of July next, but every purchaser of land sold at public sale thereafter, shall, on the day of purchase, make complete payment therefore; and the purchaser at private sale shall produce, to the register of the land office, a receipt from the treasurer of the United States, or from the receiver of public moneys of the district, for the amount of the purchase money on any tract, before he shall enter the same at the land office . . .

SEC. 3. *And be it further enacted,* That from and after the first day of July next, the price at which the public

[8] *U. S. Statutes at Large,* Vol. 3 (1850), 17th Congress, 1st Session, Ch. 51, pp. 566-567.

lands shall be offered for sale, shall be one dollar and twenty-five cents an acre; and at every public sale, the highest bidder, who shall make payment as aforesaid, shall be the purchaser; but no land shall be sold, either at public or private sale, for a less price than one dollar and twenty-five cents an acre; and all the public lands which shall have been offered at public sale before the first day of July next, and which shall then remain unsold, as well as the lands that shall thereafter be offered at public sale, according to law, and remain unsold at the close of such public sales, shall be subject to be sold at private sale, by entry at the land office, at one dollar and twenty-five cents an acre, to be paid at the time of making such entry as aforesaid . . .

SEC. 4. *And be it further enacted,* That no lands which have reverted, or which shall hereafter revert, and become forfeited to the United States for failure in any manner to make payment, shall, after the first day of July next, be subject to entry at private sale, nor until the same shall have been first offered to the highest bidder at public sale . . .

— 10 —

JACKSON'S MAYSVILLE ROAD
VETO, MAY 27, 1830[9]

The construction of a national highway (the Cumberland Road) was authorized by Congress in 1806 and begun in 1811. Its first leg (from the Potomac to the Ohio) was opened to traffic in 1818. Building was continued until 1852 when the road—passing through Columbus, Ohio, and Indianapolis, Indiana—reached Vandalia, Illinois. In 1830, however, President Andrew Jackson put a stop to the building of branches to the National Road, as his veto of the Maysville Road bill indicates. In fact, his veto ended Federal appropriations for road-building for more than half a century. (See below, Document 27.)

✓   ✓   ✓

Independently of the sanction given to appropriations for the Cumberland and other roads and objects under this power, the Administration of Mr. Madison was characterized by an act which furnishes the strongest evidence of his opinion of its extent. A bill was passed through both Houses of Congress and presented for his approval, "setting apart and pledging certain funds for constructing roads and canals and improving the navigation of water courses, in order to facilitate, promote, and give security to internal commerce among the several States and to render more easy and less expensive the means and provisions for the common defense." Regarding the bill as asserting a power in the Federal Government to construct roads and canals within the limits of the States in which

[9] Richardson, James, ed., *Messages and Papers of the Presidents*, Vol. 2, pp. 483-489.

they were made, he objected to its passage on the ground
of its unconstitutionality, declaring that the assent of the
respective States in the mode provided by the bill could
not confer the power in question; that the only cases in
which the consent and cession of particular States can
extend the power of Congress are those specified and provided for in the Constitution, and superadding to these
avowals his opinion that "a restriction of the power 'to
provide for the common defense and general welfare' to
cases which are to be provided for by the expenditure
of money would still leave within the legislative power of
Congress all the great and most important measures of
Government, money being the ordinary and necessary
means of carrying them into execution." I have not been
able to consider these declarations in any other point of
view than as a concession that the right of appropriation
is not limited by the power to carry into effect the measure
for which the money is asked, as was formerly contended.

The views of Mr. Monroe upon this subject were not
left to inference. During his Administration a bill was
passed through both Houses of Congress conferring the
jurisdiction and prescribing the mode by which the Federal Government should exercise it in the case of the
Cumberland road. He returned it with objections to its
passage, and in assigning them took occasion to say that
in the early stages of the Government he had inclined to
the construction that it had no right to expend money except in the performance of acts authorized by the other
specific grants of power, according to a strict construction
of them, but that on further reflection and observation his
mind had undergone a change; that his opinion then was
"that Congress have an unlimited power to raise money,
and that in its appropriation they have a discretionary
power, restricted only by the duty to appropriate it to purposes of common defense, and of general, not local, national, not State, benefit;" and this was avowed to be the
governing principle through the residue of his Administration. . . .

This brief reference to known facts will be sufficient to
show the difficulty, if not impracticability, of bringing back
the operations of the Government to the construction of
the Constitution set up in 1798, assuming that to be its

true reading in relation to the power under consideration, thus giving an admonitory proof of the force of implication and the necessity of guarding the Constitution with sleepless vigilance against the authority of precedents which have not the sanction of its most plainly defined powers; for although it is the duty of all to look to that sacred instrument instead of the statute book, to repudiate at all times encroachments upon its spirit, which are too apt to be effected by the conjuncture of peculiar and facilitating circumstances, it is not less true that the public good and the nature of our political institutions require that individual differences should yield to a well-settled acquiescence of the people and confederated authorities in particular constructions of the Constitution on doubtful points. Not to concede this much to the spirit of our institutions would impair their stability and defeat the objects of the Constitution itself.

The bill before me does not call for a more definite opinion upon the particular circumstances which will warrant appropriations of money by Congress to aid works of internal improvement, for although the extension of the power to apply money beyond that of carrying into effect the object for which it is appropriated has, as we have seen, been long claimed and exercised by the Federal Government, yet such grants have always been professedly under the control of the general principle that the works which might be thus aided should be "of a general, not local, national, not State," character. A disregard of this distinction would of necessity lead to the subversion of the federal system. That even this is an unsafe one, arbitrary in its nature, and liable, consequently, to great abuses, is too obvious to require the confirmation of experience. It is, however, sufficiently definite and imperative to my mind to forbid my approbation of any bill having the character of the one under consideration. I have given to its provisions all the reflection demanded by a just regard for the interests of those of our fellow-citizens who have desired its passage, and by the respect which is due to a coordinate branch of the Government, but I am not able to view it in any other light than as a measure of purely local character; or, if it can be considered national, that no further distinction between the appropriate duties of the General and State Governments need be attempted, for there can be no local interest that may not with equal propriety be denominated national. It has no connection with any established system of improvements; is exclusively within the limits of a State, starting at a point on the Ohio River and running out 60 miles to an interior town, and even as far as the State is interested conferring partial instead of general advantages. . . .

What is properly *national* in its character or otherwise is an inquiry which is often extremely difficult of solution. The appropriations of one year for an object which is considered national may be rendered nugatory by the refusal of a succeeding Congress to continue the work on the ground that it is local. No aid can be derived from the intervention of corporations. The question regards the character of the work, not that of those by whom it is to be accomplished. Notwithstanding the union of the Government with the corporation by whose immediate agency any work of internal improvement is carried on, the inquiry will still remain, Is it national and conducive to the benefit of the whole, or local and operating only to the advantage of a portion of the Union?

But although I might not feel it to be my official duty to interpose the Executive veto to the passage of a bill appropriating money for the construction of such works as are authorized by the States and are national in their character, I do not wish to be understood as expressing an opinion that it is expedient at this time for the General Government to embark in a system of this kind; and anxious that my constituents should be possessed of my views on this as well as on all other subjects which they have committed to my discretion, I shall state them frankly and briefly. Besides many minor considerations, there are two prominent views of the subject which have made a deep impression upon my mind, which, I think, are well entitled to your serious attention, and will, I hope, be maturely weighed by the people.

From the official communication submitted to you it appears that if no adverse and unforeseen contingency happens in our foreign relations and no unusual diversion be made of the funds set apart for the payment of the national debt we may look with confidence to its entire ex-

tinguishment in the short period of four years. The extent
to which this pleasing anticipation is dependent upon the
policy which may be pursued in relation to measures of
the character of the one now under consideration must be
obvious to all, and equally so that the events of the present
session are well calculated to awaken public solicitude
upon the subject. By the statement from the Treasury
Department and those from the clerks of the Senate and
House of Representatives, herewith submitted, it appears
that the bills which have passed into laws, and those which
in all probability will pass before the adjournment of Congress, anticipate appropriations which, with the ordinary
expenditures for the support of Government, will exceed
considerably the amount in the Treasury for the year 1830.
Thus, whilst we are diminishing the revenue by a reduction of the duties on tea, coffee, and cocoa the appropriations for internal improvement are increasing beyond the
available means of the Treasury. And if to this calculation
be added the amounts contained in bills which are pending
before the two Houses, it may be safely affirmed that $10,-
000,000 would not make up the excess over the Treasury
receipts, unless the payment of the national debt be post-
poned and the means now pledged to that object applied
to those ennumerated in these bills. Without a well-regu-
lated system of internal improvement this exhausting mode
of appropriation is not likely to be avoided, and the plain
consequence must be either a continuance of the national
debt or a resort to additional taxes.

Although many of the States, with a laudable zeal and
under the influence of an enlightened policy, are successfully applying their separate efforts to works of this character, the desire to enlist the aid of the General Government in the construction of such as from their nature ought
to devolve upon it, and to which the means of the individual States are inadequate, is both rational and patriotic,
and if that desire is not gratified now it does not follow
that it never will be. The general intelligence and public
spirit of the American people furnish a sure guaranty that
at the proper time this policy will be made to prevail under
circumstances more auspicious to its successful prosecution
than those which now exist. But great as this object undoubtedly is, it is not the only one which demands the foster-

ing care of the Government. The preservation and success
of the republican principle rest with us. To elevate its character and extend its influence rank among our most important duties, and the best means to accomplish this desirable end are those which will rivet the attachment of our
citizens to the Government of their choice by the comparative lightness of their public burthens and by the attraction
which the superior success of its operations will present to
the admiration and respect of the world. . . .

— 11 —

JACKSON'S VETO OF THE BANK BILL, JULY 10, 1832[10]

Andrew Jackson was hostile to the Bank of the United States—indeed, he was opposed to all banks because he believed that the only currency circulating ought to be hard money. The result was that when the friends of the Bank sought to renew its charter in 1832 (it was not to terminate until 1836) Jackson intervened and vetoed the bill. His attitude toward banking in general, his fear of foreign influence, and his broad and unsubstantiated charges of "monopoly" are clearly revealed in the message he sent to the Senate. His final statement reveals the essentially equalitarian nature of Jacksonian democracy. His veto was not overriden; and when the Bank was made the leading issue of the presidential campaign of that year and Jackson won, the Bank was doomed. Jackson withdrew the Government deposits from the Bank; the States chartered many new State banks; and the controlling hand of the Bank of the United States on unchecked speculation and unredeemable bank notes was gone. Order in banking was not restored until the passage of the National Banking Act of 1863 and 1864; central banking did not reappear until the creation of the Federal Reserve System in 1914.

The bill "to modify and continue" the act entitled "An act to incorporate the subscribers to the Bank of the United States" was presented to me on the 4th July instant. Having considered it with that solemn regard to the principles of the Constitution which the day was cal-

[10] Richardson, James, ed., *Messages and Papers of the Presidents,* Vol. 2, pp. 576-589.

culated to inspire, and come to the conclusion that it ought not to become a law, I herewith return it to the Senate, in which it originated, with my objections.

A bank of the United States is in many respects convenient for the Government and useful to the people. Entertaining this opinion, and deeply impressed with the belief that some of the powers and privileges possessed by the existing bank are unauthorized by the Constitution, subversive of the rights of the States, and dangerous to the liberties of the people, I felt it my duty at an early period of my Administration to call the attention of Congress to the practicability of organizing an institution combining all its advantages and obviating these objections. I sincerely regret that in the act before me I can perceive none of those modifications of the bank charter which are necessary, in my opinion, to make it compatible with justice, with sound policy, or with the Constitution of our country.

The present corporate body, denominated the president, directors, and company of the Bank of the United States, will have existed at the time this act is intended to take effect twenty years. It enjoys an exclusive privilege of banking under the authority of the General Government, a monopoly of its favor and support, and, as a necessary consequence, almost a monopoly of the foreign and domestic exchange. The powers, privileges, and favors bestowed upon it in the original charter, by increasing the value of the stock far above its par value, operated as a gratuity of many millions to the stockholders. . . .

Every monopoly and all exclusive privileges are granted at the expense of the public, which ought to receive a fair equivalent. The many millions which this act proposes to bestow on the stockholders of the existing bank must come directly or indirectly out of the earnings of the American people. It is due to them, therefore, if their Government sell monopolies and exclusive privileges, that they should at least exact for them as much as they are worth in open market. The value of the monopoly in this case may be correctly ascertained. The twenty-eight millions of stock would probably be at an advance of 50 per cent, and command in market at least $42,000,000, subject to the payment of the present bonus. The present value of the monopoly, therefore, is $17,000,000, and this the act proposes to sell for three millions, payable in fifteen annual installments of $200,000 each. . . .

But this act does not permit competition in the purchase of this monopoly. It seems to be predicated on the erroneous idea that the present stockholders have a prescriptive right not only to the favor but to the bounty of Government. It appears that more than a fourth part of the stock is held by foreigners and the residue is held by a few hundred of our own citizens, chiefly of the richest class. For their benefit does this act exclude the whole American people from competition in the purchase of this monopoly and dispose of it for many millions less than it is worth. This seems the less excusable because some of our citizens not now stockholders petitioned that the door of competition might be opened, and offered to take a charter on terms much more favorable to the Government and country. . . .

It has been urged as an argument in favor of rechartering the present bank that the calling in its loans will produce great embarrassment and disaster. . . . To acknowledge (the force of this reason) is to admit that the bank ought to be perpetual and as a consequence, the present stockholders and those inheriting their rights as successors be established a privileged order, clothed both with great political power and enjoying immense pecuniary advantages from their connection with the Government. . . .

(Of the $28 million of privately owned stock, $8 million are held abroad, $13 million are in the East, $5 million are in the South, and less than $250,000 are in the West.) As little stock is held in the West, it is obvious that the debt of the people in that section to the bank is principally a debt to the Eastern and foreign stockholders; that the interest they pay upon it is carried into the Eastern States and into Europe, and that it is a burden upon their industry and a drain of their currency, which no country can bear without inconvenience and occasional distress. To meet this burden and equalize the exchange operations of the bank, the amount of specie drawn from those States through its branches within the last two years, as shown by its official reports, was about $6,000,000. More than half a million of this amount does not stop in the Eastern States, but passes on to Europe to pay the dividends of the foreign stockholders. In the principle of taxation recognized by this act the Western States find no adequate compensation for this perpetual burden on their industry and drain of their currency. The branch bank at Mobile made last year $95,140, yet under the provisions of this act the State of Alabama can raise no revenue from these profitable operations, because not a share of the stock is held by any of her citizens. Mississippi and Missouri are in the same condition in relation to the branches at Natchez and St. Louis, and such, in a greater or less degree, is the condition of every Western State. The tendency of the plan of taxation which this act proposes will be to place the whole United States in the same relation to foreign countries which the Western States now bear to the Eastern. When by a tax on resident stockholders the stock of this bank is made worth 10 or 15 per cent more to foreigners than to residents, most of it will inevitably leave the country.

Thus will this provision in its practical effect deprive the Eastern as well as the Southern and Western States of the means of raising a revenue from the extension of business and great profits of this institution. It will make the American people debtors to aliens in nearly the whole amount due to this bank, and send across the Atlantic from two to five millions of specie every year to pay the bank dividends.

In another of its bearings this provision is fraught with danger. Of the twenty-five directors of this bank five are chosen by the Government and twenty by the citizen stockholders. From all voice in these elections the foreign stockholders are excluded by the charter. In proportion, therefore, as the stock is transferred to foreign holders the extent of suffrage in the choice of directors is curtailed. Already is almost a third of the stock in foreign hands and not represented in elections. It is constantly passing out of the country, and this act will accelerate its departure. . . .

Is there no danger to our liberty and independence in a bank that in its nature has so little to bind it to our country? The president of the bank has told us that most of the State banks exist by its forbearance. Should its influence become concentered, as it may under the operation of such an act as this, in the hands of a self-elected directory whose interests are identified with those of the foreign stockholders, will there not be cause to tremble for the purity of our elections in peace and for the independence of our country in war? Their power would be great whenever they might choose to exert it; but if this monopoly were regularly renewed every fifteen or twenty years on terms proposed by themselves, they might seldom in peace put forth their strength to influence elections or control the affairs of the nation. But if any private citizen or public functionary should interpose to curtail its powers or prevent a renewal of its privileges, it can not be doubted that he would be made to feel its influence. . . .

If we must have a bank with private stockholders, every consideration of sound policy and every impulse of American feeling admonishes that it should be *purely American*. Its stockholders should be composed exclusively of our own citizens, who at least ought to be friendly to our Government and willing to support it in times of difficulty and danger. So abundant is domestic capital that competition in subscribing for the stock of local banks has recently led almost to riots. To a bank exclusively of American stockholders, possessing the powers and privileges granted by this act, subscriptions for $200,000,000 could be readily obtained. Instead of sending abroad the stock of the bank in which the Government must deposit its funds and on which it must rely to sustain its credit in times of emergency, it would rather seem to be expedient to prohibit its sale to aliens under penalty of absolute forfeiture. . . .

The old Bank of the United States possessed a capital of only $11 million, which was found fully sufficient to enable it with dispatch and safety to perform all the functions required of it by the Government. The capital of the present bank is $35 million—at least twenty-four more than experience has proved necessary to enable a bank to perform its public functions. The public debt which existed during the period of the old bank and on the establishment of the new has been nearly paid off, and our revenue will soon be reduced. This increase of capital is therefore not for public but for private purposes. . . .

Upon what principle, then, are the banking establishments of the Bank of the United States and their usual banking operations to be exempted from taxation? It is not their public agency or the deposits of the Government which the States claim a right to tax, but their banks and their banking powers, instituted and exercised within State jurisdiction for their private emolument—those powers and privileges for which they pay a bonus, and which the States tax in their own banks. The exercise of these powers within a State, no matter by whom or under what authority, whether by private citizens in their original right, by corporate bodies created by the States, by foreigners or the agents of foreign governments located within their limits, forms a legitimate object of State taxation. From this and like sources, from the persons, property, and business that are found residing, located, or carried on under their jurisdiction, must the States, since the surrender of their right to raise a revenue from imports and exports, draw all the money necessary for the support of their governments and the maintenance of their independence. There is no more appropriate subject of taxation than banks, banking, and bank stocks, and none to which the States ought more pertinaciously to cling.

It can not be *necessary* to the character of the bank as a fiscal agent of the Government that its private business should be exempted from that taxation to which all the State banks are liable, nor can I conceive it *"proper"* that the substantive and most essential powers reserved by the States shall be thus attacked and annihilated as a means of executing the powers delegated to the General Government. It may be safely assumed that none of those sages who had an agency in forming or adopting our Constitution ever imagined that any portion of the taxing power of the States not prohibited to them nor delegated to Congress was to be swept away and annihiliated as a means of executing certain powers delegated to Congress. . . .

Thus may our own powers and the rights of States, which we can not directly curtail or invade, be frittered away and extinguished in the use of means employed by us to execute other powers. That a bank of the United States, competent to all the duties which may be required by the Government, might be so organized as not to infringe on our own delegated powers or the reserved rights of the States I do not entertain a doubt. Had the Executive been called upon to furnish the project of such an institution, the duty would have been cheerfully performed. In the absence of such a call it was obviously proper that he should confine himself to pointing out those prominent features in the act presented which in his opinion make it incompatible with the Constitution and sound policy. A general discussion will now take place, eliciting new light and settling important principles; and a new Congress, elected in the midst of such discussion, and furnishing an equal representation of the people according to the last census, will bear to the Capitol the verdict of public opinion, and, I doubt not, bring this important question to a satisfactory result.

Under such circumstances the bank comes forward and asks a renewal of its charter for a term of fifteen years upon conditions which not only operate as a gratuity to the stockholders of many millions of dollars, but will sanction any abuses and legalize any encroachments.

Suspicions are entertained and charges are made of gross abuse and violation of its charter. An investigation unwillingly conceded and so restricted in time as necessarily to make it incomplete and unsatisfactory discloses enough to excite suspicion and alarm. In the practices of the principal bank partially unveiled, in the absence of important witnesses, and in numerous charges confidently made and as yet wholly uninvestigated there was enough to induce a majority of the committee of investigation—a committee which was selected from the most able and honorable members of the House of Representatives—to recommend a suspension of further action upon the bill and a prosecution of the inquiry. As the charter had yet four years to run, and as a renewal now was not necessary to the successful prosecution of its business, it was to have been expected that the bank itself, conscious of its purity and proud of its character, would have withdrawn its application for the present, and demanded the severest scrutiny into all its transactions. In their declining to do so there seems to be an additional reason why the functionaries of the Government should proceed with less haste and more caution in the renewal of their monopoly. . . .

It is to be regretted that the rich and powerful too often bend the acts of government to their selfish purposes. Distinctions in society will always exist under every just government. Equality of talents, of education, or of wealth cannot be produced by human institutions. In the full enjoyment of the gifts of Heaven and the fruits of superior industry, economy, and virtue, every man is equally entitled to protection by law; but when the laws undertake to add to these natural and just advantages artificial distinctions, to grant titles, gratuities, and exclusive privileges, to make the rich richer and the potent more powerful, the humble members of society—the farmers, mechanics, and laborers—who have neither the time nor the means of securing like favors for themselves, have a right to complain of the injustice of their Government. There are no necessary evils in Government. Its evils exist only in its abuses. If it would confine itself to equal protection, and as Heaven does its rain, shower its favors alike on the high and the low, the rich and the poor, it would be an unqualified blessing.

— 12 —

THE PREEMPTION ACT OF SEPTEMBER 4, 1841 [11]

The cash-payment system encouraged squatters to enter the public lands, and from time to time Congress passed special preemption laws to protect their rights. It was not until 1841 that prospective preemption was granted—that is, anyone could enter the surveyed public lands, erect an improvement, and subsequently purchase the holding (a quarter section) at the minimum price of $1.25 an acre. The right of preemption continued until 1891.

SEC. 10. *And be it further enacted,* That from and after the passage of this act, every person being the head of a family, or widow, or single man, over the age of twenty-one years, and being a citizen of the United States, or having filed his declaration of intention to become a citizen, as required by the naturalization laws, who since the first day of June, A.D. eighteen hundred and forty, has made or shall hereafter make a settlement in person on the public lands to which the Indian title had been at the time of such settlement extinguished, and which has been, or shall have been, surveyed prior thereto, and who shall inhabit and improve the same, and who has or shall erect a dwelling thereon, shall be, and is hereby, authorized to enter with the register of the land office for the district in which such land may lie, by legal subdivisions, any number of acres not exceeding one hundred and sixty, or a quarter section of land, to include the residence of such

[11] *U. S. Statutes at Large,* Vol. 5 (1850), 27th Congress, 1st Session, Ch. 6.

claimant, upon paying to the United States the minimum price of such land, subject, however, to the following limitations and exceptions: No person shall be entitled to more than one pre-emptive right by virtue of this act; no person who is the proprietor of three hundred and twenty acres of land in any State or Territory of the United States, and no person who shall quit or abandon his residence on his own land to reside on the public land in the same State or Territory, shall acquire any right of pre-emption under this act; no lands included in any reservation, by any treaty, law, or proclamation of the President of the United States, or reserved for salines, or for other purposes; no lands reserved for the support of schools, nor the lands acquired by either of the two last treaties with the Miami tribe of Indians in the State of Indiana, or which may be acquired of the Wyandot tribe of Indians in the State of Ohio, or other Indian reservation to which the title has been or may be extinguished by the United States at any time during the operation of this act; no sections of land reserved to the United States alternate to other sections granted to any of the States for the construction of any canal, railroad, or other public improvement; no sections or fractions of sections included within the limits of any incorporated town; no portions of the public lands which have been selected as the site for a city or town; no parcel or lot of land actually settled and occupied for the purposes of trade and not agriculture; and no lands on which are situated any known salines or mines, shall be liable to entry under and by virtue of the provisions of this act. . . .

SEC. 11. *And be it further enacted,* That when two or more persons shall have settled on the same quarter section of land, the right of pre-emption shall be in him or her who made the first settlement, provided such persons shall conform to the other provisions of this act; and all questions as to the right of pre-emption arising between different settlers shall be settled by the register and receiver of the district within which the land is situated, subject to an appeal to and a revision by the Secretary of the Treasury of the United States.

SEC. 12. *And be it further enacted,* That prior to any entries being made under and by virtue of the provisions of this act, proof of the settlement and improvement thereby required, shall be made to the satisfaction of the register and receiver of the land district in which such lands may lie . . .

SEC. 13. *And be it further enacted,* That before any person claiming the benefit of this act shall be allowed to enter such lands, he or she shall make oath before the receiver or register of the land district in which the land is situated, (who are hereby authorized to administer the same,) that he or she has never had the benefit of any right of pre-emption under this act; that he or she is not the owner of three hundred and twenty acres of land in any State or Territory of the United States, nor hath he or she settled upon and improved said land to sell the same on speculation, but in good faith to appropriate it to his or her own exclusive use or benefit; and that he or she has not, directly or indirectly, made any agreement or contract, in any way or manner, with any person or persons whatsoever, by which the title which he or she might acquire from the Government of the United States, should enure in whole or in part, to the benefit of any person except himself or herself. . . .

13

COMMONWEALTH VERSUS HUNT, MARCH, 1842 [12]

This was the first effort, on the part of a State court, to prevent the use of the common law rule against conspiracy to stop workers from organizing and employing the strike to better their conditions. Chief Justice Lemuel Shaw, who wrote it, declared that neither combinations of workers nor their striking for a closed shop were in themselves unlawful conspiracies. It took almost a hundred years, however, before the ruling had a universal application.

✦   ✦   ✦

SHAW, C. J. . . . The general rule of the common law is that it is a criminal and indictable offense for two or more to confederate and combine together, by concerted means, to do that which is unlawful or criminal, to the injury of the public, or portions or classes of the community, or even to the rights of an individual. This rule of law may be equally in force as a rule of the common law, in England and in this commonwealth; and yet it must depend upon the local laws of each country to determine, whether the purpose to be accomplished by the combination, or the concerted means of accomplishing it, be unlawful or criminal in the respective countries. . . .

. . . Stripped then of these introductory recitals and alleged injurious consequences, and of the qualifying epithets attached to the facts, the averment is this; that the defendants and others formed themselves into a society, and agreed not to work for any person, who should employ any journeyman or other person, not a member of such society, after notice given him to discharge such workman.

The manifest intent of the association is, to induce all those engaged in the same occupation to become members of it. Such a purpose is not unlawful. It would give them a power which might be exerted for useful and honorable purposes, or for dangerous and pernicious ones. If the latter were the real and actual object, and susceptible of proof, it should have been specially charged. Such an association might be used to afford each other assistance in times of poverty, sickness and distress; or to raise their intellectual, moral and social condition; or to make improvement in their art; or for other proper purposes. Or the association might be designed for purposes of oppression and injustice. But in order to charge all those, who become members of an association, with the guilt of a criminal conspiracy, it must be averred and proved that the actual, if not the avowed object of the association, was criminal. An association may be formed, the declared objects of which are innocent and laudable, and yet they may have secret articles, or an agreement communicated only to the members, by which they are banded together for purposes injurious to the peace of society or the rights of its members. Such would undoubtedly be a criminal conspiracy, on proof of the fact, however meritorious and praiseworthy the declared objects might be. The law is not to be hoodwinked by colorable pretences. It looks at truth and reality, through whatever disguise it may assume. But to make such an association, ostensibly innocent, the subject of prosecution as a criminal conspiracy, the secret agreement, which makes it so, is to be averred and proved as the gist of the offence. But when an association is formed for purposes actually innocent, and afterwards its powers are abused, by those who have the control and management of it, to purposes of oppression and injustice, it will be criminal in those who thus misuse it, or give consent thereto, but not in the other members of the association. In this case, no such secret agreement, varying the objects of the association from those avowed, is set forth in this count of the indictment.

Nor can we perceive that the objects of this association, whatever they may have been, were to be attained by criminal means. The means which they proposed to employ, as averred in this count, and which, as we are now to presume, were established by the proof, were, that they would not work for a person, who, after due notice, should employ a journeyman not a member of their society. Supposing the object of the association to be laudable and lawful, or at least not unlawful, are these means criminal? The case supposes that these persons are not bound by contract, but free to work for whom they please, or not to work, if they so prefer. In this state of things, we cannot perceive, that it is criminal for men to agree together to exercise their own acknowledged rights, in such a manner as best to subserve their own interests. One way to test this is, to consider the effect of such an agreement, where the object of the association is acknowledged on all hands to be a laudable one. Suppose a class of workmen, impressed with the manifold evils of intemperance, should agree with each other not to work in a shop in which ardent spirit was furnished, or not to work in a shop with any one who used it, or not to work for an employer, who should, after notice, employ a journeyman who habitually used it. The consequences might be the same. A workman, who should still persist in the use of ardent spirit, would find it more difficult to get employment; a master employing such an one might, at times, experience inconvenience in his work, in losing the services of a skilful but intemperate workman. Still it seems to us, that as the object would be lawful, and the means not unlawful, such an agreement could not be pronounced a criminal conspiracy.

From this count in the indictment, we do not understand that the agreement was, that the defendants would refuse to work for an employer, to whom they were bound by contract for a certain time, in violation of that contract; nor that they would insist that an employer should discharge a workman engaged by contract for a certain time, in violation of such contract. It is perfectly consistent with every thing stated in this count, that the effect of the agreement was, that when they were free to act, they would not engage with an employer, or continue in his employment, if such employer, when free to act, should engage with a workman, or continue a workman in his employment, not a member of the association. If a large number of men, engaged for a certain time, should combine together to violate their contract, and quit their employment together, it would present a very different question. Suppose a farmer, employing a large number of men, engaged for the year, at fair monthly wages, and suppose that just at the moment that his crops were ready to harvest, they should all combine to quit his service, unless he would advance their wages, at a time when other laborers could not be obtained. It would surely be a conspiracy to do an unlawful act, though of such a character, that if done by an individual, it would lay the foundation of a civil action only, and not of a criminal prosecution. It would be a case very different from that stated in this count.

The second count, omitting the recital of unlawful intent and evil disposition, and omitting the direct averment of an unlawful club or society, alleges that the defendants, with others unknown, did assemble, conspire, confederate and agree together, not to work for any master or person who should employ any workman not being a member of a certain club, society or combination, called the Boston Journeymen Bootmaker's Society, or who should break any of their by-laws, unless such workmen should pay to said club, such sum as should be agreed upon as a penalty for the breach of such unlawful rules, &c; and that by means of said conspiracy they did compel one Isaac B. Wait, a master cordwainer, to turn out of his employ one Jeremiah Horne, a journeyman boot-maker, &c. in evil example, &c. So far as the averment of a conspiracy is concerned, all the remarks made in reference to the first count are equally applicable to this. It is simply an averment of an agreement amongst themselves not to work for a person, who should employ any person not a member of a certain association. It sets forth no illegal or criminal purpose to be accomplished, nor any illegal or criminal means to be adopted for the accomplishment of any purpose. It was an agreement, as to the manner in which they would exercise an acknowledged right to contract with others for their labor. It does not aver a conspiracy or even an intention to raise their wages, and it appears by the bill of exceptions that the case was not put upon the footing of a conspiracy to raise their wages. . . .

We think, therefore, that associations may be entered

into, the object of which is to adopt measures that may have a tendency to impoverish another, that is, to diminish his gains and profits, and yet so far from being criminal or unlawful, the object may be highly meritorious and public spirited. The legality of such an association will therefore depend upon the means to be used for its accomplishment. If it is to be carried into effect by fair or honorable and lawful means, it is, to say the least, innocent; if by falsehood or force, it may be stamped with the character of conspiracy. It follows as a necessary consequence, that if criminal and indictable, it is so by reason of the criminal means intended to be employed for its accomplishment; and as a further legal consequence, that as the criminality will depend on the means, those means must be stated in the indictment. . . .

It appears by the bill of exceptions, that it was contended on the part of the defendants, that this indictment did not set forth any agreement to do a criminal act, or to do any lawful act by criminal means, and that the agreement therein set forth did not constitute a conspiracy indictable by the law of this State, and that the court was requested so to instruct the jury. This the court declined doing, but instructed the jury that the indictment did describe a confederacy among the defendants to do an unlawful act, and to effect the same by unlawful means—that the society, organized and associated for the purposes described in the indictment, was an unlawful conspiracy against the laws of this State, and that if the jury believed, from the evidence, that the defendants or any of them had engaged in such confederacy, they were bound to find such of them guilty.

In this opinion of the learned judge, this court, for the reason stated, cannot concur. Whatever illegal purpose can be found in the constitution of the Bootmakers' Society, it not being clearly set forth in the indictment, cannot be relied upon to support this conviction. So if any facts were disclosed at the trial, which, if properly averred, would have given a different character to the indictment, they do not appear in the bill of exceptions, nor could they, after verdict, aid the indictment. But looking solely at the indictment, disregarding the qualifying epithets, recitals and immaterial allegations, and confining ourselves to facts so averred as to be capable of being traversed and put in issue, we cannot perceive that it charges a criminal conspiracy punishable by law. The exceptions must, therefore, be sustained, and the judgment arrested. . . .

— 14 —

PRELIMINARY REPORT OF THE EIGHTH CENSUS, 1860[13]

With pardonable pride, the Census Bureau was able to report the great advances American manufactures had made during the decade 1850-1860. The total value of domestic manufactures (including fisheries and the products of the mines) had been $1,019,106,616 in 1850; by June 1, 1860, this had increased to $1,900,000,000, or more than 86 per cent. Below are selected passages from the Census Report, relating particularly to the growing use of machinery, the use of coal, the impact of the sewing machine on ready-to-wear clothing and the development of the cotton-goods, boots and shoes, and watches industries.

✓   ✓   ✓

Probably no class of statistics possesses more general interest, as illustrating the recent progress of the country in all the operative branches, and in mechanical engineering, than those relating to MACHINERY. Nearly every section of the country, particularly the Atlantic slope, possesses a great affluence of water power, which has been extensively appropriated for various manufacturing purposes. The construction of hydraulic machinery, of stationary and locomotive steam-engines, and all the machinery used in mines, mills, furnaces, forges, and factories; in the building of roads, bridges, canals, railways, &c.; and for all other purposes of the engineer and manufacturer, has become a pursuit of great magnitude. The annual product of the general machinists' and millwrights' establishments,

[13] *Eighth Census of the U. S.* (Washington, May 19, 1862), pp. 62-69.

as returned in the census of 1850, was valued at $27,998,-344. The value of the same branch, exclusive of sewing-machines, amounted in 1860 to $47,118,550, an increase of over eighteen millions in ten years. The middle States were the largest producers, having made over 48 per cent. of the whole, but the southern and western States exhibit the largest relative increase. The ratio of increase in the several sections was as follows: New England, 16.4 per cent.; middle States, 55.2; southern, 387; and western, 127 per cent. The Pacific States produced machinery of the value of $1,686,510, of which California made $1,600,510. In Rhode Island the business was slightly diminished, but in Connecticut it had increased 165 per centum. The great facilities possessed by New York and Pennsylvania in iron, coal, and transportation, made them the largest manufacturers of machinery, which in the former was made to the value of $10,484,863, and in the latter, $7,243,453—an increase of 24.4 and 75 per cent., respectively. New Jersey raised her product to $3,215,673, an increase of 261 per cent., while Delaware and Maryland and the District of Columbia exhibited an increase of 82, 41, and 667 per cent., respectively. In all the southern States the value of the manufacture, though small, was largely increased; the ratio in Virginia, the largest producer, being 236 per cent., while in Mississippi, Alabama, and South Carolina, the next in amount of production, it was 1,626,270, and 525 per centum, respectively. This was exclusive of cotton-gins, which were included with agricultural machinery. Ohio was the largest producer in the west, and the fourth in the Union, having made to the value of $4,855,005, an increase of 125 per cent. on the product of 1850. Kentucky ranked next among the western States, having produced over one million dollars' worth, and increased her product 213 per cent. The ratio of increase in the other western States was, in Indiana, 98; in Illinois, 24; Wisconsin, 208; Missouri, 214; and Iowa, 2,910 per cent, respectively; but in Michigan there was a small decrease in the amount manufactured.

Besides a large amount of machinery and other castings included in the returns of machine shops, the value of the production of IRON FOUNDERIES, returned by the census of 1860, reached the sum of $27,970,193, an increase of 42 per cent. on the value of that branch in 1850, which was $20,111,517. New York, whose extensive stove founderies swell the amount of production in that State, made to the value of $8,216,124, and Pennsylvania, $4,977,793, an increase of 39 and 60.9 per cent., respectively.

With the subject of iron and its various manufactures that of FOSSIL FUEL naturally associates itself. The unequalled wealth and rapid development of the coal fields of the United States as a dynamic element in our industrial progress affords one of the most striking evidences of our recent advance. The product of all the coal mines of the United States, in 1850, was valued at $7,173,750. The annual value of the anthracite and bituminous coal, according to the Eighth Census, was *over nineteen millions* of dollars. The increase was over twelve millions of dollars, and was at the rate of 169.9 per cent. on the product of 1850. It was chiefly produced in Pennsylvania, Ohio, and Virginia. The coal mined in Pennsylvania, in 1850, was valued at $5,268,351. In the year ending June 1, 1860, the State produced 9,397,332 tons of anthracite, worth $11,869,574, and of bituminous coal, 66,994,295 bushels, valued at $2,833,859, making a total value of $14,703,433, or an excess of $7,529,683 over the total product of the Union in 1850. Of bituminous coal, Ohio raised 28,339,900 bushels, the value of which was $1,539,713; and Virginia, 9,542,627 bushels, worth $690,188. The increase in Ohio was $819,587, and in Virginia, $222,780, in the value of mineral fuel, being at the rate of 113 per cent. in the former, and 47.6 per cent. in the latter. The increase in Pennsylvania was 179 per centum on the yield of 1850.

The development of our several valuable mines of coal, iron, lead, copper, zinc, gold, silver, quicksilver, chrome, &c., is a subject of the highest satisfaction, constituting, as they do, the repository and fountainhead of crude materials for an immense and varied industry in the metallurgic and chemical arts. Mining in its several branches employs a very large amount of capital and great numbers of our laborious population, and shows a steady increase in the last ten years. The product of the gold mines in the Atlantic States has, however, fallen off since the discoveries of gold in California. . . .

The SEWING MACHINE has also been improved and

introduced, in the last ten years, to an extent which has made it altogether a revolutionary instrument. It has opened avenues to profitable and healthful industry for thousands of industrious females to whom the labors of the needle had become wholly unremunerative and injurious in their effects. Like all automatic powers, it has enhanced the comforts of every class by cheapening the process of manufacture of numerous articles of prime necessity, without permanently subtracting from the average means of support of any portion of the community. It has added a positive increment to the permanent wealth of the country by creating larger and more varied applications of capital and skill in the several branches to which it is auxiliary. The manufacture of the machines has itself become one of considerable magnitude, and has received a remarkable impulse since 1850. The returns show an aggregate of 116,330 machines made in nine States in 1860, the value of which was $5,605,345. A single establishment in Connecticut manufactured machines to the value of over $2,700,000, or nearly one-half of the whole production in that year. During the year 1861 sewing-machines to the value of over $61,000 were exported to foreign countries. It is already employed in a great variety of operations and upon different materials, and is rapidly becoming an indispensable and general appendage to the household.

Among the branches of industry which have been signally promoted by the introduction of the sewing-machine is the manufacture of men's and women's CLOTHING for sale, which has heretofore ranked with the cotton manufactures in the number of hands—two-thirds of them females—and the cost of labor employed. The increase of this manufacture has been general throughout the Union, and in the four cities of New York, Philadelphia, Cincinnati, and Boston, amounted in value to nearly forty and one-quarter millions of dollars, or over 83 per cent. of the product of the whole Union in 1850. The manufacture of shirts and collars, of ladies' cloaks and mantillas—a new branch which has received its principal impulse within the last ten years—and of ladies' and gentlemen's furnishing goods generally, form very large items in the general aggregate of this branch. They severally employ extensive and numerous establishments, many of them in our large cities with heavy capital. In Troy, New York, the value of shirt collars alone annually manufactured is nearly $800,000, approximating in value to the product of the numerous and extensive iron founderies which have been a source of wealth to that city.

The influence of improved machinery is also conspicuously exhibited in the manufacture of SAWED and PLANED LUMBER, in which the United States stands altogether unrivalled, as well for the extent and perfection of the mechanism employed as the amount of the product. This reached, in 1850, the value of $58,521,976, and, in 1860, $95,912,286, an increase of 64 per cent. in the last decade. The western States alone, in the latter year, produced lumber to the value of $33,274,793, an increase of $18,697,543, or 128 per cent. over their manufacture in 1850. The Pacific States and Territories produced to the value of $6,-171,431, and the southern $17,941,162, a respective increase of $3,841,826 and $9,094,686 in those sections, being a ratio of 162.7 and 102.3 per centum.

Several branches of manufacture have an intimate relation to agriculture and the landed interests, and by their extension powerfully promote those interests as well as that of commerce. Surpassing all others of this or any other class in the value of products and of the raw material consumed, is the manufacture of flour and meal. The product of FLOUR and GRIST MILLS in 1850 reached a value of nearly one hundred and thirty-six millions of dollars, while in 1860 the returns exhibit a value of $223,144,369—an increase of $87,246,563, or 64.2 per cent. in the last ten years. . . .

Among the great branches of pure manufacture in the United States, that of COTTON GOODS holds the first rank in respect to the value of the product and the amount of capital employed. Aided by the possession of the raw material as a product of our own soil, and by the enterprise and ingenuity of our people, this valuable industry has grown with a rapidity almost unrivalled.

The total value of cotton goods manufactured in New England was $80,301,535, and in the middle States $26,-272,111—an increase of 83.4 per cent. in the former, and 77.7 in the latter. The remaining States produced to the value of $8,564,280, making the whole production during that year $115,137,926 against $65,501,687, the value of this branch in 1850, or an increase in the general business of nearly 76 per centum in 10 years. . . .

The manufacture of BOOTS and SHOES employs a larger number of operatives than any other single branch of American industry. The census of 1850 showed that there were 11,305 establishments, with a capital of nearly thirteen millions of dollars, engaged in making boots and shoes to the value of $53,967,408, and employing 72,305 male and 32,948 female hands. The returns of 1860 show that 2,554 establishments in the New England States employed a capital only $2,516 less than that of the whole Union at the former date; and with 56,039 male and 24,978 female employés produced boots and shoes of the value of $54,-767,077 or eight hundred thousand dollars more than the entire value of the business in 1850, and 82.8 per centum in excess of their own production in that year. Massachusetts increased 92.6 per cent., having made boots and shoes of the value of $46,440,209, equal to 86.8 per cent. of the general business in 1850. The State of New York returned 2,276 factories, with an aggregate production of $10,878,-707; and New England, New York, Pennsylvania, and New Jersey together produced $75,674,946 worth of these articles, being 40.4 per cent. more than the product of all the States in 1850, and 67.9 per cent. more than their own manufacture in that year. The three counties of Essex, Worcester, and Plymouth, in Massachusetts, produced boots and shoes to the value severally of about 14½, 9½, 9¼ millions of dollars. The largest production of any one town was that of Philadelphia, in which it amounted to $5,329,-887; the next that of Lynn, Massachusetts, was $4,867,399; the third, Haverhill, $4,130,500; the fourth, New York city, $3,869,068. The largest production of a single establishment was of one in North Brookfield, Massachusetts, and amounted to over $750,000. This establishment was the largest of five the same proprietors had in operation that year, the total production whereof was over one million pairs of boots and shoes, valued at more than thirteen hundred thousand dollars! Machinery propelled by steam power is now used in many large manufactories with highly satisfactory results. . . .

The manufacture of American WATCHES, commenced

within the last ten years in Boston as an experiment, has proved eminently successful. Unable, heretofore to compete with the low-priced labor of European workmen, our ingenious countrymen have perfected machinery, by the aid of which watch movements are fabricated equal, if not superior, to the hand-made. The continued growth of this branch will diminish the importation of foreign watches, and may, at no distant period, earn for our country a reputation in this manufacture equal to that she enjoys in the kindred branch of clock-making. Gold and silver watch cases are now produced to a very large extent, chiefly in the cities of Philadelphia, New York, and Newark. . . .

15

THE TARIFF ACT OF MARCH 2, 1861[14]

The first protective tariff of modern times—which, in fact, showed the way until the Smoot-Hawley Tariff of 1930—was the act of 1861, introduced and enacted before the Civil War broke out. Justin S. Morrill, who introduced the bill in the House, said the intention was only to restore the rates of 1846; but the act was openly protectionist because in many cases it substituted specific for ad valorem duties and raised these duties, particularly on iron and on wool. The Act was called "An Act to Provide for the Payment of Outstanding Treasury Notes, to Authorize a Loan, to Regulate and Fix the Duties on Imports and for Other Purposes." It was amended repeatedly during the Civil War years so that the Tariff Act of 1864 put the average rate on dutiable commodities up to 47 per cent. The iron and woolen schedules are given here as examples of the detailed kind of tariff-making that Congress engaged in.

SEC. 7. *And be it further enacted*, That from and after the day and year aforesaid there shall be levied, collected, and paid, on the importation of the articles hereinafter mentioned, the following duties, that is to say:

First: On bar-iron, rolled or hammered, comprising flats not less than one inch, or more than seven inches wide, nor less than one quarter of an inch or more than two inches thick; rounds, not less than one-half an inch or more than four inches in diameter; and squares not less than one-

[14] *U. S. Statutes at Large*, Vol. 12, 36th Congress, 2nd Session, Ch. 68, pp. 180-185.

half an inch or more than four inches square, fifteen dollars per ton: *Provided,* That all iron in slabs, blooms, loops or other forms, less finished than iron in bars and more advanced than pig-iron, except castings, shall be rated as iron in bars, and pay a duty accordingly: *And provided, further,* That none of the above iron shall pay a less rate of duty than twenty per centum ad valorem; on all iron imported in bars for railroads or inclined planes made to patterns and fitted to be laid down upon such roads or planes without further manufacture and not exceeding six inches high, twelve dollars per ton; on boiler plate iron, twenty dollars per ton; on iron wire drawn and finished, not more than one-fourth of one inch in diameter nor less than number sixteen wire gauge, seventy-five cents per one hundred pounds, and fifteen per centum ad valorem; over number sixteen and not over number twenty-five wire gauge, one dollar and fifty cents per one hundred pounds and in addition fifteen per centum ad valorem; over or finer than number twenty-five wire gauge, two dollars per one hundred pounds and in addition fifteen per centum ad valorem; on all other descriptions of rolled or hammered iron not otherwise provided for, twenty dollars per ton.

Second: On iron in pigs, six dollars per ton; on vessels of cast-iron not otherwise provided for, and on sad-irons, tailors and hatters irons, stoves and stove plates, one cent per pound; on cast-iron steam, gas and water pipe, fifty cents per one hundred pounds; on cast-iron butts and hinges, two cents per pound; on hollow-ware, glazed or tinned, two cents and a half per pound; on all other castings of iron not otherwise provided for, twenty-five per centum ad valorem.

Third: On old scrap iron, six dollars per ton: *Provided,* That nothing shall be deemed old iron that has not been in actual use and fit only to be remanufactured.

Fourth: On band and hoop iron, slit rods not otherwise provided for, twenty dollars per ton; on cut nails and spikes, one cent per pound; on iron cables or chains, or parts thereof, and anvils, one dollar and twenty-five cents per one hundred pounds; on anchors, or parts thereof, one dollar and fifty cents per one hundred pounds; on wrought board nails, spikes, rivets, and bolts, two cents per pound; on bed screws and wrought hinges, one cent and a half per pound; on chains, trace chains, halter chains, and fence chains made of wire or rods one-half of one inch in diameter or over, one cent and a half per pound; under one-half of one inch in diameter, and not under one-fourth of one inch in diameter, two cents per pound; under one-fourth of one inch in diameter, and not under number nine wire gauge, two cents and a half per pound; under number nine wire gauge, twenty-five per centum ad valorem; on blacksmiths' hammers and sledges, axles or parts thereof, and malleable iron in castings not otherwise provided for, two cents per pound; on horse-shoe nails, three cents and a half per pound; on steam, gas, and water tubes and flues of wrought iron, two cents per pound; on wrought iron railroad chairs and on wrought iron nuts and washers, ready punched, twenty-five dollars per ton; on cut tacks, brads, and sprigs not exceeding sixteen ounces to the thousand, two cents per thousand; exceeding sixteen ounces to the thousand, two cents per pound.

Fifth: On smooth or polished sheet iron by whatever name designated, two cents per pound; on other sheet iron, common or black not thinner than number twenty wire gauge, twenty dollars per ton; thinner than number twenty and not thinner than number twenty-five wire gauge, twenty-five dollars per ton; thinner than number twenty-five wire gauge, thirty dollars per ton; on tin plates galvanized, galvanized iron, or iron coated with zinc, two cents per pound; on mill irons and mill cranks of wrought iron, and wrought iron for ships, locomotives, locomotive tire, or parts thereof, and steam engines, or parts thereof, weighing each twenty-five pounds or more, one cent and a half per pound; on screws commonly called wood screws, two inches or over in length, five cents per pound; less than two inches in length, eight cents per pound; on screws washed or plated, and all other screws of iron or any other metal, thirty per centum ad valorem; on all manufactures of iron not otherwise provided for, thirty per centum ad valorem.

Sixth: On all steel in ingots, bars, sheets, or wire not less than one fourth of one inch in diameter, valued at seven cents per pound or less, one and a half cent per pound; valued at above seven cents per pound and not above eleven cents per pound, two cents per pound; steel in any form not otherwise provided for, shall pay a duty of twenty per centum ad valorem . . .

SEC. 13. *And be it further enacted,* That from and after the day and year aforesaid, there shall be levied, collected, and paid on the importation of the articles hereinafter mentioned the following duties, that is to say:

First: On Wilton, Saxony and Aubusson, Axminster patent velvet, Tournay velvet, and tapestry velvet carpets and carpeting, Brussels carpets wrought by the Jacquard machine, and all medallion or whole carpets, valued at one dollar and twenty-five cents or under per square yard, forty cents per square yard; valued at over one dollar and twenty-five cents per square yard, fifty cents per square yard: *Provided,* That no carpet or rugs of the above description shall pay a duty less than twenty-five per centum ad valorem; on Brussels and tapestry Brussels carpets and carpeting printed on the warp or otherwise, thirty cents per square yard; on all treble-ingrain and worsted-chain Venetian carpets and carpeting, twenty-five cents per square yard; on hemp or jute carpeting, four cents per square yard; on druggets, bockings, and felt carpets and carpeting printed, colored or otherwise, twenty cents per square yard; on all other kinds of carpets and carpeting of wool, flax or cotton, or parts of either, or other material not otherwise specified, a duty of thirty per centum ad valorem; *Provided,* That mats, rugs, screens, covers, hassocks, bedsides and other portions of carpets or carpeting shall pay the rate of duty herein imposed on carpets or carpeting of similar character; on all other mats, screens, hassocks, and rugs, a duty of thirty per centum ad valorem.

Second: On woollen cloths, woollen shawls, and all manufactures of wool of every description, made wholly or in part of wool, not otherwise provided for, a duty of twelve cents per pound, and in addition thereto twenty-five per centum ad valorem; on endless belts for paper, and blanketing for printing machines, twenty-five per centum ad valorem; on all flannels valued at thirty cents or less per square yard, twenty-five per centum ad valorem; valued above thirty cents per square yard, and on all flannels colored, printed, or plaided, and flannels composed in part of cotton or silk, thirty per centum ad valorem; on hats of wool, twenty per centum ad valorem; on woollen and worsted yarn, valued at fifty cents and not over one dollar per pound, twelve cents per pound, and in addition thereto fifteen per centum ad valorem; on woollen and worsted yarn, valued at over one dollar per pound, twelve cents per pound, and in addition thereto twenty-five per centum ad valorem; on woollen and worsted yarns, or yarns for carpets, valued under fifty cents per pound, and not exceeding in fineness number fourteen, twenty-five per centum ad valorem; exceeding number fourteen, thirty per centum ad valorem; on clothing ready made, and wearing apparel of every description, composed wholly or in part of wool, made up or manufactured wholly or in part by the tailor, seamstress, or manufacturer, twelve cents per pound, and in addition thereto twenty-five per centum ad valorem; on blankets of all kinds, made wholly or in part of wool, valued at not exceeding twenty-eight cents per pound, there shall be charged a duty of six cents per pound, and in addition thereto ten per centum ad valorem; on all valued above twenty-eight cents per pound, but not exceeding forty cents per pound, there shall be charged a duty of six cents per pound, and in addition thereto twenty-five per centum ad valorem; on all valued above forty cents per pound there shall be charged a duty of twelve cents per pound, and in addition thereto twenty per centum ad valorem; on woollen shawls, or shawls of which wool shall be the chief component material, a duty of sixteen cents per pound, and in addition thereto twenty per centum ad valorem.

Third: On all delaines, Cashmere delaines, muslin delaines, barege delaines, composed wholly or in part of wool, gray or uncolored, and on all other gray or uncolored goods of similar description, twenty-five per centum ad valorem; on bunting, and on all stained, colored, or printed, and on all other manufactures of wool, or of which wool shall be a component material, not otherwise provided for, thirty per centum ad valorem.

Fourth: On oil-cloth, for floors, stamped, painted, or printed, valued at fifty cents or less per square yard, twenty per centum ad valorem; valued at over fifty cents per square yard, and on all other oil-cloth, thirty per centum ad valorem.

SEC. 14. *And be it further enacted,* That from and after the day and year aforesaid, there shall be levied, collected, and paid on the importation of the articles hereinafter mentioned the following duties, that is to say:

First: On all manufactures of cotton not bleached, colored, stained, painted, or printed, and not exceeding one hundred threads to the square inch, counting the warp and filling, and exceeding in weight five ounces per square yard, one cent per square yard; on finer or lighter goods of like description, not exceeding one hundred and forty threads to the square inch, counting the warp and filling, two cents per square yard; on goods of like description, exceeding one hundred and forty threads, and not exceeding two hundred threads to the square inch, counting the warp and filling, three cents per square yard; on like goods exceeding two hundred threads to the square inch, counting the warp and filling, four cents per square yard; on all goods embraced in the foregoing schedules, if bleached, there shall be levied, collected, and paid an additional duty of one-half of one cent per square yard; and if printed, painted, colored, or stained, there shall be levied, collected, and paid a duty of ten per centum in addition to the rates of duty provided in the foregoing schedules: *Provided,* That upon all plain woven cotton goods not included in the foregoing schedules, and upon cotton goods of every description, the value of which shall exceed sixteen cents per square yard, there shall be levied, collected, and paid a duty of twenty-five per centum ad valorem: *And provided, further,* That no cotton goods having more than two hundred threads to the square inch, counting the warp and filling, shall be admitted to a less rate of duty than is provided for goods which are of that number of threads.

Second: On spool and other thread of cotton, thirty per centum ad valorem.

Third: On shirts and drawers, wove or made on frames composed wholly of cotton and cotton velvet, twenty-five per centum ad valorem; and on all manufactures composed wholly of cotton, bleached, unbleached, printed, painted, or dyed, not otherwise provided for, thirty per centum ad valorem.

Fourth: On all brown or bleached linens, ducks, canvas

paddings, cot-bottoms, burlaps, drills, coatings, brown Hollands, blay linens, damasks, diapers, crash, huckabacks, handkerchiefs, lawns, or other manufactures of flax, jute, or hemp, [or of which flax, jute, or hemp] shall be the component material of chief value, being of the value of thirty cents and under per square yard, twenty-five per centum ad valorem. . . .

16

THE HOMESTEAD ACT OF
MAY 20, 1862[15]

After long agitation—and the espousal of the proposal by the Republican party in 1856 and again in 1860—a Homestead Law was passed in 1862 to make possible free entry into the public lands. Despite the high hopes held for it, the law was not able to curb the activities of land speculators or encourage large numbers to become homesteaders. In fact, by the turn of the century, not much more than one-tenth of those who completed their entries had started by being homesteaders.

✓   ✓   ✓

Be it enacted by the Senate and House of Representatives of the United States of America in Congress assembled, That any person who is the head of a family, or who has arrived at the age of twenty-one years, and is a citizen of the United States, or who shall have filed his declaration of intention to become such, as required by the naturalization laws of the United States, and who has never borne arms against the United States Government or given aid and comfort to its enemies, shall, from and after the first January, eighteen hundred and sixty-three, be entitled to enter one quarter section or a less quantity of unappropriated public lands, upon which said person may have filed a preëmption claim, or which may, at the time the application is made, be subject to preëmption at one dollar and twenty-five cents, or less, per acre; or eighty acres or less of such unappropriated lands, at two

[15] *U. S. Statutes at Large,* Vol. 12, 37th Congress, 2nd Session, Ch. 75.

dollars and fifty cents per acre, to be located in a body, in conformity to the legal subdivisions of the public lands, and after the same shall have been surveyed: *Provided,* That any person owning and residing on land may, under the provisions of this act, enter other land lying contiguous to his or her said land, which shall not, with the land so already owned and occupied, exceed in the aggregate one hundred and sixty acres.

SEC. 2. *And be it further enacted,* That the person applying for the benefit of this act shall, upon application to the register of the land office in which he or she is about to make such entry, make affidavit . . . that such application is made for his or her exclusive use and benefit, and that said entry is made for the purpose of actual settlement and cultivation, and not either directly or indirectly for the use or benefit of any other person or persons whomsoever; and upon filing the said affidavit with the register or receiver, and on payment of ten dollars, he or she shall thereupon be permitted to enter the quantity of land specified: *Provided, however,* That no certificate shall be given or patent issued therefor until the expiration of five years from the date of such entry; and if, at the expiration of such time, or at any time within two years thereafter, the person making such entry; or, if he be dead, his widow; or in case of her death, his heirs or devisee; or in case of a widow making such entry, her heirs or devisee, in case of her death; shall prove by two credible witnesses that he, she, or they have resided upon or cultivated the same for the term of five years immediately succeeding the time of filing the affidavit aforesaid, and shall make affidavit that no part of said land has been alienated, and that he has borne true allegiance to the Government of the United States; then, in such case, he, she, or they, if at that time a citizen of the United States, shall be entitled to a patent, as in other cases provided for by law: *And provided, further,* That in case of the death of both father and mother, leaving an infant child, or children, under twenty-one years of age, the right and fee shall enure to the benefit of said infant child or children; and the executor, administrator, or guardian may, at any time within two years after the death of the surviving parent, and in accordance with the laws of the State in which such children for the time being have their domicil, sell said land for the benefit of said infants, but for no other purpose; and the purchaser shall acquire the absolute title by the purchase, and be entitled to a patent from the United States, on payment of the office fees and sum of money herein specified. . . .

SEC. 4. *And be it further enacted,* That no lands acquired under the provisions of this act shall in any event become liable to the satisfaction of any debt or debts contracted prior to the issuing of the patent therefor.

SEC. 5. *And be it further enacted,* That if, at any time after the filing of the affidavit, as required in the second section of this act, and before the expiration of the five years aforesaid, it shall be proven, after due notice to the settler, to the satisfaction of the register of the land office, that the person having filed such affidavit shall have actually changed his or her residence, or abandoned the said land for more than six months at any time, then and in that event the land so entered shall revert to the government.

SEC. 6. *And be it further enacted,* That no individual shall be permitted to acquire title to more than one quarter section under the provisions of this act. . . . *Provided,* That nothing contained in this act shall be so construed as to impair or interfere in any manner whatever with existing preëmption rights: *And provided, further,* That all persons who may have filed their applications for a preëmption right prior to the passage of this act, shall be entitled to all privileges of this act: *Provided, further,* That no person who has served, or may hereafter serve, for a period of not less than fourteen days in the army or navy of the United States, either regular or volunteer, under the laws thereof, during the existence of an actual war, domestic or foreign, shall be deprived of the benefits of this act on account of not having attained the age of twenty-one years. . . .

SEC. 8. *And be it further enacted,* That nothing in this act shall be so construed as to prevent any person who has availed him or herself of the benefits of the first section of this act, from paying the minimum price, or the price to which the same may have graduated, for the quantity of land so entered at any time before the expiration of the five years, and obtaining a patent therefor from the government, as in other cases provided by law, on making proof of settlement and cultivation as provided by existing laws granting preëmption rights.

— 17 —

THE PACIFIC RAILWAY ACT OF JULY 1, 1862[16]

The building of a Pacific railway had agitated the country during the 1850's; but Southern objections prevented Congress from acting. The Republican party was committed to the project and, when the Civil War was raging, it found the time to authorize the Federal incorporation of companies to build such a line. The Union Pacific and the Central Pacific Railroads thus appeared; and with Federal support—in land grants and loans—the road to the Pacific was built. This pattern of Federal assistance was responsible for granting more than 115,000,000 acres of the public domain and lending more than $60,000,000 to land-grant railroads during the years 1862-1873.

🖝   🖝   🖝

. . . The said corporation is hereby authorized and empowered to lay out, locate, construct, furnish, maintain, and enjoy a continuous railroad and telegraph, with the appurtenances, from a point on the one hundredth meridian of longitude west from Greenwich, between the south margin of the valley of the Republican River and the north margin of the valley of the Platte River, in the Territory of Nebraska, to the western boundary of Nevada Territory, upon the route and terms hereinafter provided, and is hereby vested with all the powers, privileges, and immunities necessary to carry into effect the purposes of this act as herein set forth. The capital stock of said company shall consist of one hundred thousand shares of one thousand

---

[16] *U. S. Statutes at Large,* Vol. 12, 37th Congress, 2nd Session, Ch. 120, pp. 490-497.

dollars each, which shall be subscribed for and held in not more than two hundred shares by any one person, and shall be transferable in such manner as the by-laws of said corporation shall provide. The persons hereinbefore named, together with those to be appointed by the Secretary of the Interior, are hereby constituted and appointed commissioners, and such body shall be called the Board of Commissioners of the Union Pacific Railroad and Telegraph Company, and twenty-five shall constitute a quorum for the transaction of business. . . .

SEC. 2. *And be it further enacted,* That the right of way through the public lands be, and the same is hereby, granted to said company for the construction of said railroad and telegraph line; and the right, power, and authority is hereby given to said company to take from the public lands adjacent to the line of said road, earth, stone, timber, and other materials for the construction thereof; said right of way is granted to said railroad to the extent of two hundred feet in width on each side of said railroad where it may pass over the public lands, including all necessary grounds for stations, buildings, workshops, and depots, machine shops, switches, side tracks, turntables, and water stations. The United States shall extinguish as rapidly as may be the Indian titles to all lands falling under the operation of this act and required for the said right of way and grants hereinafter made.

SEC. 3. *And be it further enacted,* That there be, and is hereby, granted to the said company, for the purpose of aiding in the construction of said railroad and telegraph line, and to secure the safe and speedy transportation of the mails, troops, munitions of war, and public stores thereon, every alternate section of public land, designated by odd numbers, to the amount of five alternate sections per mile on each side of said railroad, on the line thereof, and within the limits of ten miles on each side of said road, not sold, reserved, or otherwise disposed of by the United States, and to which a preëmption or homestead claim may not have attached, at the time the line of said road is definitely fixed: *Provided,* That all mineral lands shall be excepted from the operation of this act; but where the same shall contain timber, the timber thereon is hereby granted to said company. And all such lands, so granted by this section, which shall not be sold or disposed of by said company within three years after the entire road shall have been completed, shall be subject to settlement and preëmption, like other lands, at a price not exceeding one dollar and twenty-five cents per acre, to be paid to said company. . . .

SEC. 5. *And be it further enacted,* That for the purposes herein mentioned the Secretary of the Treasury shall, upon the certificate in writing of said commissioners of the completion and equipment of forty consecutive miles of said railroad and telegraph, in accordance with the provisions of this act, issue to said company bonds of the United States of one thousand dollars each, payable in thirty years after date, bearing six per centum per annum interest, (said interest payable semi-annually,) which interest may be paid in United States treasury notes or any other money or currency which the United States have or shall declare lawful money and a legal tender, to the amount of sixteen of said bonds per mile for such section of forty miles; and to secure the repayment to the United States, as hereinafter provided, of the amount of said bonds so issued and delivered to said company, together with all interest thereon which shall have been paid by the United States, the issue of said bonds and delivery to the company shall ipso facto constitute a first mortgage on the whole line of the railroad and telegraph, together with the rolling stock, fixtures and property of every kind and description, and in consideration of which said bonds may be issued; and on the refusal or failure of said company to redeem said bonds, or any part of them, when required so to do by the Secretary of the Treasury, in accordance with the provisions of this act, the said road, with all the rights, functions, immunities, and appurtenances thereunto belonging, and also all lands granted to the said company by the United States, which, at the time of said default, shall remain in the ownership of the said company, may be taken possession of by the Secretary of the Treasury, for the use and benefit of the United States: *Provided,* This section shall not apply to that part of any road now constructed. . . .

SEC. 9. . . . The Central Pacific Railroad Company of California, a corporation existing under the laws of the

State of California, are hereby authorized to construct a railroad and telegraph line from the Pacific coast, at or near San Francisco, or the navigable waters of the Sacramento River, to the eastern boundary of California, upon the same terms and conditions, in all respects, as are contained in this act for the construction of said railroad and telegraph line first mentioned, and to meet and connect with the first mentioned railroad and telegraph line on the eastern boundary of California. . . .

SEC. 11. *And be it further enacted,* That for three hundred miles of said road most mountainous and difficult of construction, to wit: one hundred and fifty miles westwardly from the eastern base of the Rocky Mountains, and one hundred and fifty miles eastwardly from the western base of the Sierra Nevada mountains, said points to be fixed by the President of the United States, the bonds to be issued to aid in the construction thereof shall be treble the number per mile hereinbefore provided, and the same shall be issued, and the lands herein granted be set apart, upon the construction of every twenty miles thereof, upon the certificate of the commissioners as aforesaid that twenty consecutive miles of the same are completed; and between the sections last named of one hundred and fifty miles each, the bonds to be issued to aid in the construction thereof shall be double the number per mile first mentioned, and the same shall be issued, and the lands herein granted be set apart, upon the construction of every twenty miles thereof, upon the certificate of the commissioners as aforesaid that twenty consecutive miles of the same are completed: *Provided,* That no more than fifty thousand of said bonds shall be issued under this act to aid in constructing the main line of said railroad and telegraph. . . .

SEC. 18. *And be it further enacted,* That whenever it appears that the net earnings of the entire road and telegraph, including the amount allowed for services rendered for the United States, after deducting all expenditures, including repairs, and the furnishing, running, and managing of said road, shall exceed ten per centum upon its cost, exclusive of the five per centum to be paid to the United States, Congress may reduce the rates of fare thereon, if unreasonable in amount, and may fix and establish the same by law. And the better to accomplish the object of this act, namely, to promote the public interest and welfare by the construction of said railroad and telegraph line, and keeping the same in working order, and to secure to the government at all times (but particularly in time of war) the use and benefits of the same for postal, military and other purposes, Congress may, at any time, having due regard for the rights of said companies named herein, add to, alter, amend, or repeal this act. . . .

— 18 —

SENATOR SHERMAN ON THE NATIONAL BANKING ACT OF FEBRUARY 10, 1863 [17]

At the behest of Secretary of the Treasury Chase, Senator John Sherman sponsored and became the outstanding advocate of the National Banking Act of 1863. His speech is an excellent statement of the monetary situation of the country as a result of the Civil War and incorporates the hope that the new National Banks would create some order out of the chaos which was already developing.

✓   ✓   ✓

Mr. SHERMAN. Mr. President, the importance of the subject under consideration demands a fuller statement than has yet been made of the principles and objects of this bill. I wished to avoid the labor of discussing this subject; but it seems to be necessary. I shall endeavor to condense what I have to say, for I know the time of the Senate is precious, and I desire to get a vote on this bill, if practicable, to-day.

It is the misfortune of war that we are compelled to act upon measures of grave importance without that mature deliberation secured in peaceful times. We are now to act upon a measure that will affect the property of every citizen of the United States, and yet our action for good or evil must be concluded within the few days or weeks of this session. We are about to choose between a permanent system, designed to establish a uniform national currency, based upon the public credit, limited in amount, and

[17] *Congressional Globe,* 37th Congress, 3rd Session, pp. 840-846.

guarded by all the restraints which the experience of men has proved necessary, and a system of paper money, without limit as to amount, except for the growing necessities of war. In the consideration of such a question we surely should sacrifice all local interests, all pride of opinions; and, while acting promptly under the pressure of events, we should bring to our aid all the wisdom of united counsels, and all the light which the experience of former generations of men can give us. . . .

It must be remembered that this bill is taken up when our financial condition is not the most favorable. Gold is at a premium of between fifty and sixty per cent., and is substantially banished from circulation. We are in the midst of war, when the necessities of the Government require us to have large sums of money. We cannot choose as to the mode in which we shall get that money. If we pursue the ordinary course, the course that has been sufficient in times of peace to raise money, of putting our bonds into market and selling them for what they will bring, it would be at a great sacrifice. We know this from the history of other nations and from our own experience. We, therefore, must look to some system of finance that will give us all the aid possible either in the form of paper money or by the agencies of associated banks. We know very well that after this war is over, this Government will still be largely in need of money; that when the rebellion is subdued, the condition of society in the southern States will be disturbed; that it will be necessary to maintain for some time considerable armies in order to preserve peace; and that in any aspect of affairs this Government must undertake responsibilities and incur debts and liabilities of which we have had no example in our previous history.

The financial measures heretofore adopted are necessary to be considered before I proceed to examine the features of this bill. After the war broke out we were able to borrow money upon the credit of the United States until December, 1861. The amount of demand notes previously issued was comparatively small. In December, 1861, by the suspension of specie payments the whole of the gold was withdrawn from circulation, and there was nothing then in circulation but the paper of local banks, which by the laws of the United States could not be used in Government transactions. We were then in the peculiar condition of a nation involved in war without any currency whatever which by law could be used in the ordinary transactions of the public business. Gold was withdrawn by the suspension of specie payments; the money of the banks could not be used because the laws of the United States forbade it; and we were without any currency whatever.

Under these circumstances Congress wisely authorized the issue of a considerable sum of United States notes. That this measure was wise but few will controvert. We were compelled by a necessity as urgent as could be imposed upon any legislature to issue these notes. To the extent to which they were issued they were useful. They were eagerly sought by our people. They were taken by our enemies in the South, by our friends in the North. They were taken in the East and in the West. They furnished the best substitute for gold and silver that could then be devised; and if we would limit the United States notes to the amount now authorized by law they would form a stable and valuable currency.

But, sir, we know, not only by our own experience, but by the experience of other nations, that when a Government issues paper money in very large amounts, and without connecting it in any way with the private operations of the people, it inevitably depreciates, and, if carried to excess, deranges the values of all property. Still necessity presses us for money, and most of the great nations of modern times have during war been compelled by necessity to resort to some form of paper money. It has always been the most difficult problem of war to maintain the Government credit and yet to procure the very large sums indispensable for its prosecution. We have but four expedients from which to choose: first, to repeal the sub-Treasury act, and use the paper of local banks as a currency; secondly, to increase largely the issue of United States notes; thirdly, to organize a system of national banking; or, fourthly, to sell the bonds of the United States in the open market. . . .

Another practical objection to these United States notes is, that there is no mode of redemption. They are safe; they are of uniform value; but there is no mode pointed out by which they are to be redeemed. No one is bound to redeem them. They are receivable, but not convertible. They are debts of the United States, but they cannot be presented anywhere for redemption. No man can present them, except for the purpose of funding them into the bonds of the United States. They are not convertible; they lack that essential element of any currency.

Another objection is, that they can only be used during the war. The very moment that peace comes, all this circulation that now fills the channels of commercial operations will be at once banished. They will be converted into bonds; and then the contraction of prices will be as rapid as the inflation has been. The issue of Government notes can only be a temporary measure, and is only intended as a temporary measure to provide for a national exigency.

Another serious objection to these notes is, that they are made the basis of bank issues. Under the operation of the act declaring them to be a legal tender, the bank circulation has increased from $120,000,000 to $167,000,000. The banks have sold their gold at a large premium, and placed in their vaults United States notes with which to redeem their own notes. That cannot be avoided. As we have made them a legal tender, banks are bound to take them in payment of debts due to them, and they therefore have the right to hold them to pay their debts with. The consequence has been that, while the Government has been issuing its paper money, some of the banks have also been inflating the currency by issuing paper money on the basis of United States money. . . .

The practical difficulty is, how to check inflation by banks. . . .

It would be very easy for me to prove that during war local banks are the natural enemies of a national currency. They were in the war of 1812. Whenever specie payments are suspended, the power to issue a bank note is the same as the power to coin money. If you give to an individual or a corporation the power to issue his note as money at a time when he is not restrained by the necessity of paying it in gold and silver, you give him practically the power to coin money. . . .

Sir, while I believe that no system of paper money should depend alone upon banks, I am far from objecting to their agencies. They are useful and necessary mediums of exchange, indispensable in all commercial countries. The only power they derive from incorporation not granted to all citizens is the power to issue notes as money, and this power is not necessary for their business or essential to their profit. Their business connects them with the currency; and whether it be gold or paper, they are deeply interested in its credit and value. Is it not then possible to preserve to the Government the exclusive right to issue paper money, and yet not injuriously affect the interests of the local banks?

This is the object of this bill. But it is asked, why look at all to the interests of the banks; why not directly issue the notes of the Government, and thus save to the people the interest in the debt represented by the notes in circulation?

The only answer to this question is that history teaches us that the public faith of a nation alone is not sufficient to maintain a paper currency. There must be a combination between the interests of private individuals and the Government.

Mr. President, I have thus endeavored to show that Government paper money, unsupported by private capital, cannot be maintained as a currency in time of war. I have also endeavored to show, and did show on a former occasion, that the issuing of notes by a diversity of private banks under State authority, and unchecked by specie payments, is inexpedient, destructive, and, in my opinion, unconstitutional. The two systems cannot exist together. They will inevitably induce inflation and ultimate bankruptcy. A good national currency as a substitute for gold and silver can only exist by combining the two systems; so that the Government may issue notes of uniform tenure properly secured, and the banks shall redeem and maintain their credit. . . .

Mr. President, we are already in a period of great inflation. The Government of the United States has either in circulation or has authorized now nearly four hundred million dollars of United States notes. We have a bank circulation of from one hundred and sixty to one hundred and seventy millions. If we adopt the proposition which is sent to us from the House of Representatives to go on increasing our circulation by the issue of $300,000,000 more it will create an inflation that will inevitably lead to the derangement of all the business affairs of the country. . . .

The question then occurs—the only one, indeed, which is at all practical to this discussion—whether the bank bill proposed by the Secretary of the Treasury, and introduced by me in the Senate, will tend to secure us a national currency beyond the danger of inflation. Its general provisions are no doubt known to Senators. The amount of circulation limited by the terms of this bill is $300,000,000. Is that currency safe? I think any one who will read this bill with candor will find that beyond all contingency the currency proposed to be issued under it is safe. It is first secured by the bonds of the United States; a margin of ten per cent. is left for depreciation; and then in case of further depreciation the Secretary is authorized to call for the deposit of a greater amount of bonds. While the depreciation under par exists no interest can be paid upon these bonds, but it is held in the hands of the Secretary of the Treasury for redemption. Besides that, the banks have to keep on hand twenty-five per cent. in lawful money. The Senator from Kentucky [Mr. POWELL] proposes to make that gold and silver; but that is perfectly futile and impossible now. The bank bill requires that twenty-five per cent. of all the deposits and all the circulation shall be kept on hand, so that the note-holder will first have the security of the bonds of the Government and a margin for depreciation; he will have twenty-five per cent. of the amount of circulation always on hand in the bank; and then, in addition to that, he will have the first lien on all property of the bank. . . .

Will this money be convertible? The United States notes are not convertible; that is, there is no one to pay them on demand. These bank bills are convertible. When they are presented at the counter it is the duty of the banker at once to pay them promptly in lawful money of the United States; and that money is to be restricted to the amount of the present issues or to the $50,000,000 additional authorized in this bill. They are convertible at any time.

This currency will be uniform. It will be printed by the United States. It will be of uniform size, shape, and form; so that a bank bill issued in the State of Maine will be current in California; a bank bill issued in Ohio will be current wherever our Government currency goes at all; and a bank bill issued in the State of Connecticut will be freely taken in Iowa or anywhere else. There is no limit to its convertibility. . . .

Now, Mr. President, let us see and examine a little more accurately the advantages the Government of the United States will derive from this system; because, unless the Government is to derive some benefit the system ought not to be pressed. I take it as an axiom that the United States should not issue United States notes to an amount greater than sufficient to fill the vacuum created by the withdrawal of gold, the amount of present issues. What benefit, then, does the United States obtain from this system? The first benefit is, there is a market furnished for the bonds of the United States. These banks must furnish ten per cent. more of the bonds of the United States than they receive in paper money. This at once, if the full amount is issued, which I do not anticipate within a year, will furnish a market for over three hundred and thirty million dollars of bonds; and we know very well by the laws of demand and supply, that where a demand is made for a given article the demand extends far beyond the particular want. For instance, if there is a demand in England for ten million bushels of wheat, that demand affects the price of one hundred million bushels in this country; so that the increase in the price of wheat growing out of this unexpected demand for wheat is more than twice or threefold the value of the wheat that is demanded. You make a fixed and permanent demand for United States bonds used for banking purposes, and you give a credit to $1,000,000,000 of bonds. That is the law of demand and supply. The very demand for these bonds, owing to the necessity for capitalists to keep them to base their banking upon, will make them a desirable security. When a banker wishes these bonds other persons will wish them. Every demand you make for them increases largely the value of the security.

I have no doubt—indeed I know—that within a very short time after this system is in operation, banks will be started. I know that then there will be a demand for these bonds. Many of the bonds that are now outstanding will be absorbed for banking purposes, and others will be demanded. They will be compelled to get them. Bankers will have them; other persons will have them; because, as I said before, if you make a demand for one purpose, that demand will extend to many others; and this is an important consideration. Sir, you cannot carry on this war except by the sale of your bonds. Any ingeniously contrived system to carry it on by paper money in the form of currency will be futile. Then you can only carry on your operations, as an individual or a nation, by the sale of your bonds or the use of your credit. If you have not got the money, you must borrow it; and all other schemes are idle. You may, it is true, furnish a limited amount in paper currency. When you go one step beyond that limit fixed by the laws of finance and commerce, then you destroy the value of that which you use as currency. Your power to borrow goes on indefinitely. Your business, therefore, is to make a demand for your Government securities, and thus induce the investment of the money of the people in the bonds of the United States.

Why, sir, there is in this country an ample supply of capital for all purposes. Our annual productions are shown by the census to be $1,900,000,000 a year. The aggregate wealth of this people is over $12,000,000,000. The actual capital that is now in the hands of the people, seeking and begging for investment, would carry on this war for years. There is no want of capital. It is a want of confidence, a want of system; a fear that that which the people have will fall suddenly on their hands utterly worthless. That is the real danger. This bill does furnish a market for your bonds and your securities—that credit by which alone you can carry on a Government in time of war.

But, sir, that is not all. They will furnish a medium by which the State bank paper may be gradually absorbed—not by any harsh measures. Some of the friends of local banks think this is a great scheme to break down local banks. Why, sir, as I shall show you before I am through, it is clearly the interest of every local bank of the United States to avail itself of the provisions of this law. It will no doubt operate gradually to absorb the local banks, to retire their issues by substituting in their place an issue that will be safe, uniform, and convertible in all parts of the country. I believe this system, if it has a fair trial, a fair experiment, will gradually absorb all the State banks, without deranging the currency of the country or destroying the value of the property of stockholders in banks.

Not only that. This scheme will furnish a convenient agency for the collection of your taxes. You have now in this country collectors and assessors scattered all over the country, in every district, and the people are compelled to pay taxes; some a little and some a great deal. What is the medium by which they are to be paid? At present there is no other medium except by what are called the greenbacks, the United States notes, and these notes are forced out of circulation by the superabundance of bank paper; so that a person who desires to pay your taxes is compelled to go into your market to obtain first United States demand notes by the sale or conversion of his bank paper, and then to pay his taxes. This will furnish a convenient medium by which the taxes may be paid, and as these banks will gradually extend themselves all over the country, they will be made the convenient depositories of the public money. As it is now, every collector is bound to take what paper money he gets, and hold it in his hands subject to all risks. He dare not, under our laws, deposit it with banks. He runs all the risk of fire and accident; and all the money he may have on his hands he is responsible for. He has no safe where he can deposit it. The United States Government does not furnish a safe, and it forbids him depositing in banks. Under this system all the money of the United States may be safely deposited in banks, and that deposit will be secured by the Government bonds, so that there can be no loss.

But there is another reason in favor of this measure. It will make a community of interest between the stockholders of banks, the people, and the Government. At present there is a great contrariety and a great difference of opinion; a great diversity of interests. The local banks have one interest, and the Government currency another. They are brought into contact. But, sir, by the passage of this bill you will harmonize these interests; so that every stockholder, every mechanic, every laborer who holds one of these notes will be interested in the Government—not in a local bank, but in the Government of the United States —whose faith and credit and security he will be more anxious to uphold. If this system had been spread all over this country, and these banks had been established as agencies North and South, East and West, upon the basis of national credit, I believe they would have done very much indeed to maintain the Federal Government and to prevent the great crime of secession.

But, sir, there is a still higher motive for the passage of this bill. It will promote a sentiment of nationality. There can be no doubt of it. The policy of this country ought to be to make everything national as far as possible; to nationalize our country, so that we shall love our country. If we are dependent on the United States for a currency and a medium of exchange, we shall have a broader and a more generous nationality. The want of such nationality, I believe, is one of the great evils of the times. This doctrine of State rights, which substitutes a local community—for, after all, the most powerful State is but a local community —instead of the United States of America, has been the evil of the time; and it has been that principle of State rights, that bad sentiment that has elevated State authority above the great national authority, that has been the main instrument by which our Government is sought to be overthrown.

But, Mr. President, I say that this system will be a benefit to the banks themselves, as well as to the Government. The similarity of notes all over the United States will give them a wider circulation. A note issued by a bank in Maine will have upon it precisely the same engraving, the same form, the same character, as a note issued in Iowa. They will both rest on the same basis and the same security. This very fact will give them a broader circulation. As a matter of course, now, when a note is issued in Ohio, if it straggles as far as Washington, it is discounted two per cent., although it is just as good as any other note, and is driven back by the very fact that it is at a discount. If that note bore the similitude of the United States of America, and the stamp and the guarantee which the United States gives it, it would go everywhere; and a note-holder would not care whether it were issued in Ohio, Connecticut, or California. That very similitude would give it a broader circulation, and, consequently, a more profitable circulation to the bank; it would not be returned so quickly. I have been told by gentlemen from New England that the average periods of circulation in New England is about thirty days; in New York, in the cities, it is much less; in the West it is said to be sixty days. But, sir, these notes all being the same, they may have an indefinite circulation, and the average may extend to years, instead of months or days.

There is another important advantage which the banks would derive from this system. They would be guarded against all frauds and alterations. There would be but five or six kinds of notes in the United States, instead of the great diversity that there now is. This would be a great guard. . . .

There is another advantage these banks would have. They are made by this law depositories of the public money. All the money collected by the collectors and various other Government officers would be deposited in the banks convenient or adjacent to the collector; and these deposits are the most abundant and profitable source of revenue. They would be more stable than individual deposits. They would be paid out in the form of checks and drafts, and would be there in the banks perfectly safe, secured to the Government by the United States bonds; and yet they would be a legitimate source of banking profit. Under the present system the laws forbid such a thing. Local banks cannot be made a safe depository. The experience of the past has shown that they are not safe depositories; and, therefore, this would be an advantage which the new banks would have over the old.

There is still another advantage. These notes are to be receivable for taxes due to the United States. The notes of the State banks cannot be received by any United States officer. They are dishonored and disgraced from the beginning by being refused by the national Government. The paper of these banks will be receivable for Government dues. This would be again another profitable source of circulation. . . .

Now, sir, what benefits do the people derive from this system? Those benefits may be inferred from what I have already stated. In this way the people would have a currency combining the national faith with the private stock and private credit of individuals. They would have a currency that would be safe, uniform, and convertible. They would have all that can be desired in any community: a currency limited in amount, restrained by law, governed by law, checked by the power of visitation, checked by the limitation of liabilities, safe, uniform, and convertible in every part of the country. When I see that the people of the United States can derive these advantages; when I see that the Government of the United States can derive these advantages from this system of banks, I will not hesitate for a moment, even if I am compelled as a part of the system to induce the withdrawal of local bank paper, to induce them to surrender that which cannot safely be exercised by any private individual in time of war; and that is the power to issue or to coin money; a power that should only be granted to the Government.

Mr. President, I do not wish to pursue this argument much further; but I could show, by reference to our own history, that I seek to accomplish only what all the statesmen of our country have sought to accomplish. Every party that has been organized in this country, from the foundation of the Government to this time, has, at some period of its history, sought to accomplish this object of a uniform national currency. The Federalists, under the lead of Alexander Hamilton, brought order out of chaos after the revolutionary war by the adoption of the United States Bank. They gave us for twenty years a stable currency; and without that currency the funding system, which secured the credit of the United States, could not have been adopted. It was only through the agency of the Bank of the United States, organized in some respects upon a foundation like this, upon the basis of Government securities, that our fathers were enabled to pay off the revolutionary debt—to establish that wise system by which it was gradually diminished and finally paid off. When that bank expired we had a period of confusion and disorder. We had the issues of local banks for four or five years, when the Republican party, the rivals of the old Federalists, then in power, passed a bank bill under the lead of Mr. Madison and Mr. Dallas. The arguments at those times in this very body, and in the House of Representatives, in 1815 and 1816, show that the same difficulties by which we are now surrounded then existed—a depreciated and disordered paper currency, which could only be remedied by the substitution of one national currency. That object was accomplished by the Republican party of Mr. Madison, by the incorporation of the second Bank of the United States; and for twenty years that went on in a career of almost uninterrupted prosperity. No one lost by it. However, at the expiration of the charter of the second bank, there was no longer any debt of the United States; there was no object, so far as the Government was concerned, in having any kind of paper money. All the motive for paper money had ceased, so far as the Government was concerned. The debt was paid off. It was the object then to cease to contract any further debt; and, upon the basis of the facts then existing, I believe the adoption of the sub-Treasury scheme was a wise and judicious plan. I was too young to take part in the political disputes of that time. Probably at that time, with my natural predilections, if I had taken part, I should have been opposed to the sub-Treasury scheme; but looking on it now without any feeling, I believe the adoption of the sub-Treasury scheme was wise, and in times of peace it was ample; gold and silver were abundant enough for a national currency, . . . and were it not now necessary by the operations of war to substitute some other for it, I should not be in favor of overthrowing any portion of that system.

The Democratic party, from 1837 to 1845, adopted the sub-Treasury scheme as their national currency. We now, surrounded by difficulties, surrounded by war, and in the midst of great troubles, are compelled to resort to some scheme by which to nationalize and arrange upon a secure and firm basis a national currency. Every commercial country in the world has adopted it, and it is a remarkable fact that every nation of modern times that has attempted to base its currency solely upon Government paper has utterly failed, and has eventually repudiated that currency; but when its currency has been supported, aided, and combined with local banks, when the interests of private individuals have been combined with the Government, the issues succeeded. . . .

Under the system now proposed with the sanction of the Secretary of the Treasury, the Government of the United States pays but four per cent. on the amount of bonds filed in the Department, and these banks provide a market for a greater quantity of bonds. The banks under this system will be the means and the medium by which the Government can reach the money in the hands of the people. Those who take the responsibility of defeating a measure of this kind, unless they can substitute something better in its place than the unlimited issue of paper money, will take a responsibility that I would not for my life assume. I had doubts about this system; I examined them carefully; I weighed them all, and on my responsibility I feel bound to say that, all things considered, it is the best that can be adopted under the circumstances to avoid that which will be inevitable destruction.

If this bill is defeated, and we shall go on upon the system proposed by the House of Representatives, to issue an unlimited quantity of paper money without restraint or limitation, the price of everything will rise; the produce that we use will rise, and the expenses of the Government will be largely increased. Nothing now holds the speculative chord in the city of New York except the Senate. Unless we can devise some permanent basis for a national currency, some wise financial scheme, our people will be embarked in reckless speculation. . . .

I may be like other men who have thought a great deal on a particular subject. I may give to this question an undue importance; but with me it is all important. The establishment of a national currency, and of this system, as the best that has yet been devised, appears to me all important. It is more important than the loss of a battle. In comparison with this, the fate of three million negroes held as slaves in the southern States is utterly insignificant. I would see them slaves for life as their fathers were before them, if only we could maintain our nationality. I would see them free, disenthralled, enfranchised, on their way to the country from which they came, or settled in our own land in a climate to which they are adapted, or transported anywhere else, rather than to see our nationality overthrown. I regard all those questions as entirely subordinate to this. Sir, we cannot maintain our nationality unless we establish a sound and stable financial system; and as the basis of it we must have a uniform national currency. . . .

19

THE NATIONAL BANKING ACT OF JUNE 3, 1864 [18]

The National Banking Act was passed in 1863 and re-written in 1864. It provided that National Bank Associations be created with the right of note issue up to $300 million dollars. In 1865, State bank note issues were virtually outlawed when a tax of 10 per cent was imposed upon them. These national bank notes and the Civil War greenbacks (except for a short period when silver certificates were in circulation) were the only currency in circulation until the appearance of Federal Reserve Notes in 1914.

The law also provided for the maintenance of reserves, stipulating that so-called country banks were required to "have on hand, in lawful money of the United States, an amount equal to at least 15 per cent of the aggregate amount of its notes in circulation, and of its deposits." (Sec. 31.) Seventeen reserve cities were set up, where the country banks could keep three-fifths of the 15 per cent; banks in the reserve cities were required to keep a reserve of 25 per cent. These banks in turn could keep half of their balances in banks in the central reserve city of New York. (Sec. 32.) In the 1880's, Chicago and St. Louis also were made central reserve cities.

Be it . . . That there shall be established in the Treasury Department a separate bureau (comptroller of the currency) which shall be charged with the execution of

[18] *U. S. Statutes at Large*, Vol. 13, 38th Congress, 1st Session, Ch. 106, pp. 100-105.

this and all other laws that may be passed by Congress respecting the issue and regulation of a national currency.

SEC. 5. *And be it further enacted,* That associations for carrying on the business of banking may be formed by any number of persons, not less in any case than five, who shall enter into articles of association, which shall specify in general terms the object for which the association is formed, and may contain any other provisions, not inconsistent with the provisions of this act, which the association may see fit to adopt for the regulation of the business of the association and the conduct of its affairs, which said articles shall be signed by the persons uniting to form the association, and a copy of them forwarded to the comptroller of the currency, to be filed and preserved in his office. . . .

SEC. 7. *And be it further enacted,* That no association shall be organized under this act, with a less capital than one hundred thousand dollars, nor in a city whose population exceeds fifty thousand persons, with a less capital than two hundred thousand dollars: *Provided,* That banks with a capital of not less than fifty thousand dollars may, with the approval of the Secretary of the Treasury, be organized in any place the population of which does not exceed six thousand inhabitants.

SEC. 8. *And be it further enacted,* That every association formed pursuant to the provisions of this act shall, from the date of the execution of its organization certificate, be a body corporate, but shall transact no business except such as may be incidental to its organization and necessarily preliminary, until authorized by the comptroller of the currency to commence the business of banking. . . . and exercise under this act all such incidental powers as shall be necessary to carry on the business of banking by discounting and negotiating promissory notes, drafts, bills of exchange, and other evidences of debt; by receiving deposits; by buying and selling exchange, coin, and bullion; by loaning money on personal security; by obtaining, issuing, and circulating notes according to the provisions of this act. . . .

SEC. 16. *And be it further enacted,* That every association, after having complied with the provisions of this act, preliminary to the commencement of banking business under its provisions, and before it shall be authorized to commence business, shall transfer and deliver to the treasurer of the United States any United States registered bonds bearing interest to an amount not less than thirty thousand dollars nor less than one third of the capital stock paid in, which bonds shall be deposited with the treasurer of the United States and by him safely kept in his office until the same shall be otherwise disposed of, in pursuance of the provisions of this act; and the Secretary of the Treasury is hereby authorized to receive and cancel any United States coupon bonds, and to issue in lieu thereof registered bonds of like amount, bearing a like rate of interest, and having the same time to run; and the deposit of bonds shall be, by every association, increased as its capital may be paid up or increased, so that every association shall at all times have on deposit with the treasurer registered United States bonds to the amount of at least one third of its capital stock actually paid in . . .

SEC. 20. *And be it further enacted,* That it shall be the duty of the comptroller of the currency to countersign and enter in the book, in the manner aforesaid, every transfer or assignment of any bonds held by the treasurer presented for his signature; and the comptroller shall have at all times during office hours access to the books of the treasurer, for the purpose of ascertaining the correctness of the transfer or assignment presented to him to countersign; and the treasurer shall have the like access to the book above mentioned, kept by the comptroller, during office hours, to ascertain the correctness of the entries in the same; and the comptroller shall also at all times have access to the bonds on deposit with the treasurer, to ascertain their amount and condition.

SEC. 21. *And be it further enacted,* That upon the transfer and delivery of bonds to the treasurer, as provided in the foregoing section, the association making the same shall be entitled to receive from the comptroller of the currency circulating notes of different denominations, in blank, registered and countersigned as hereinafter provided, equal in amount to ninety per centum of the current market value of the United States bonds so transferred and delivered, but not exceeding ninety per centum of the amount of said bonds at the par value thereof, if bearing interest at a rate not less than five per centum per annum; and at no time shall the total amount of such notes, issued to any such association, exceed the amount at such time actually paid in of its capital stock. . . .

20

THE CONTRACT LABOR LAW OF JULY 4, 1864[19]

In 1864, carrying out the promise of the 1860 platform, the Republican Congress passed an "Act to Encourage Immigration," which set up the federal office of a Commissioner of Immigration and provided for an emigration office in New York City. In addition, the law permitted the immigration of contract laborers whose wages could be fixed by contract for one year. In 1885, as a result of the pressure of the Knights of Labor, Congress repealed the Act.

✦ ✦ ✦

SEC. 2. *And be it further enacted,* That all contracts that shall be made by emigrants to the United States in foreign countries, in conformity to regulations that may be established by the said commissioner, whereby emigrants shall pledge the wages of their labor for a term not exceeding twelve months, to repay the expenses of their emigration, shall be held to be valid in law, and may be enforced in the courts of the United States, or of the several states and territories; and such advances, if so stipulated in the contract, and the contract be recorded in the recorder's office in the county where the emigrant shall settle, shall operate as a lien upon any land thereafter acquired by the emigrant, whether under the homestead law when the title is consummated, or on property otherwise acquired until liquidated by the emigrant; but nothing herein contained shall be deemed to authorize any contract contravening the

[19] *U. S. Statutes at Large,* Vol. 13, 38th Congress, 1st Session, Ch. 246.

Constitution of the United States, or creating in any way the relation of slavery or servitude.

SEC. 3. *And be it further enacted,* That no emigrant to the United States who shall arrive after the passage of this act shall be compulsively enrolled for military service during the existing insurrection, unless such emigrant shall voluntarily renounce under oath his allegiance to the country of his birth, and declare his intention to become a citizen of the United States.

SEC. 4. *And be it further enacted,* That there shall be established in the city of New York an office to be known as the United States Emigrant Office; and there shall be appointed, by and with the advice and consent of the Senate, an officer for said city, to be known as superintendent of immigration, at an annual salary of two thousand dollars; and the said superintendent may employ a clerk of the first class; and such superintendent shall, under the direction of the commissioner of immigration, make contracts with the different railroads and transportation companies of the United States for transportation tickets, to be furnished to such immigrants, and to be paid for by them, and shall, under such rules as may be prescribed by the commissioner of immigration, protect such immigrants from imposition and fraud, and shall furnish them such information and facilities as will enable them to proceed in the cheapest and most expeditious manner to the place of their destination. And such superintendent of immigration shall perform such other duties as may be prescribed by the commissioner of immigration: *Provided,* That the duties hereby imposed upon the superintendent in the city of New York shall not be held to effect the powers and duties of the commissioner of immigration of the State of New York; and it shall be the duty of said superintendent in the city of New York to see that the provisions of the act commonly known as the passenger act are strictly complied with, and all breaches thereof punished according to law. . . .

— 21 —

THE COINAGE ACT OF
FEBRUARY 12, 1873[20]

*The Mint Act of 1792—one of Alexander Hamilton's
important accomplishments—called for the minting of gold
and silver at a ratio of 1 to 15, the standard weight of the
gold dollar to be 27 grains and that of silver 416 grains.
In 1834, because gold had been undervalued and no gold
coinage had taken place from 1805 on, Congress fixed the
ratio at 16 to 1, with the standard silver dollar having
412½ grains and the standard gold dollar 25 8/10 grains.
This action undervalued silver, so that it disappeared from
the mint. In the 1860's, sentiment favored the dropping of
the silver dollar altogether, retaining only the so-called
trade dollar for foreign trade (based on the Mexican dollar) and not as a standard unit of account. It was in this
spirit that the Coinage Act of 1873 was passed; the only
silver dollar it provided for was the trade dollar of 420
grains. Thus, silver was demonetized, an event that was
subsequently referred to as "The Crime of 1873."*

✓   ✓   ✓

SEC. 13. That the standard for both gold and silver coins
of the United States shall be such that of one thousand
parts by weight nine hundred shall be of pure metal and
one hundred of alloy; and the alloy of the silver coins
shall be of copper, and the alloy of the gold coins shall be
of copper, or of copper and silver; but the silver shall in
no case exceed one-tenth of the whole alloy.

SEC. 14. That the gold coins of the United States shall

[20] *U. S. Statutes at Large*, Vol. 17, 42nd Congress, 3rd Session,
Ch. 131, pp. 426-427.

be a one-dollar piece, which, at the standard weight of
twenty-five and eight-tenths grains, shall be the unit of
value; a quarter-eagle, or two-and-a-half dollar piece; a
three-dollar piece; a half-eagle, or five-dollar piece; an
eagle, or ten-dollar piece; and a double eagle, or twenty-
dollar piece. And the standard weight of the gold dollar
shall be twenty-five and eight-tenths grains; of the quarter-eagle, or two-and-a-half dollar piece, sixty-four and a
half grains; of the three-dollar piece, seventy-seven and
four-tenths grains; of the half-eagle, or five-dollar piece,
one hundred and twenty-nine grains; of the eagle, or ten-
dollar piece, two hundred and fifty-eight grains; of the
double-eagle, or twenty-dollar piece, five hundred and sixteen grains; which coins shall be a legal tender in all payments at their nominal value when not below the standard
weight and limit of tolerance provided in this act for the
single piece, and, when reduced in weight, below said
standard and tolerance, shall be a legal tender at valuation in proportion to their actual weight; and any gold
coin of the United States, if reduced in weight by natural
abrasion not more than one-half of one per centum below
the standard weight prescribed by law, after a circulation
of twenty years, as shown by its date of coinage, and at
a ratable proportion for any period less than twenty years,
shall be received at their nominal value by the United
States treasury and its offices, under such regulations as
the Secretary of the Treasury may prescribe for the protection of the government against fraudulent abrasion or
other practices; and any gold coins in the treasury of the
United States reduced in weight below this limit of abrasion shall be recoined.

SEC. 15. That the silver coins of the United States shall
be a trade-dollar, a half-dollar, or fifty-cent piece, a quarter-dollar, or twenty-five cent piece, a dime, or ten-cent
piece; and the weight of the trade-dollar shall be four hundred and twenty grains troy; the weight of the half-dollar
shall be twelve grams (grammes) and one-half of a gram,
(gramme;) the quarter-dollar and the dime shall be respectively, one-half and one-fifth of the weight of said
half-dollar; and said coins shall be a legal tender at their
nominal value for any amount not exceeding five dollars
in any one payment.

SEC. 16. That the minor coins of the United States shall be a five-cent piece, a three-cent piece, and a one-cent piece, and the alloy for the five and three cent pieces shall be of copper and nickel, to be composed of three-fourths copper and one-fourth nickel, and the alloy of the one-cent piece shall be ninety-five per centum of copper and five per centum of tin and zinc, in such proportions as shall be determined by the director of the mint. The weight of the piece of five cents shall be seventy-seven and sixteen-hundredths grains, troy; of the three-cent piece, thirty grains; and of the one-cent piece, forty-eight grains; which coins shall be a legal tender, at their nominal value, for any amount not exceeding twenty-five cents in any one payment.

SEC. 17. That no coins, either of gold, silver, or minor coinage, shall hereafter be issued from the mint other than those of the denominations, standards, and weights herein set forth. . . .

SEC. 20. That any owner of gold bullion may deposit the same at any mint, to be formed into coin or bars for his benefit; but it shall be lawful to refuse any deposit of less value than one hundred dollars, or any bullion so base as to be unsuitable for the operations of the mint; and when gold and silver are combined, if either metal be in such small proportion that it cannot be separated advantageously, no allowance shall be made to the depositor for its value.

SEC. 21. That any owner of silver bullion may deposit the same at any mint, to be formed into bars, or into dollars of the weight of four hundred and twenty grains, troy, designated in this act as trade-dollars, and no deposit of silver for other coinage shall be received; but silver bullion contained in gold deposits, and separated therefrom, may be paid for in silver coin, at such valuation as may be, from time to time, established by the director of the mint.

22

WRITING OF THE INTERSTATE COMMERCE ACT, 1887[21]

The Interstate Commerce Commission recites some of the abuses in railroading that led to Federal intervention in business practices for the first time. The new law provided that all charges made by carriers should be "reasonable and just"; that rebates and pools were illegal; that charges for short hauls higher than those for long hauls "when the conditions were substantially the same" were unlawful; and that rate schedules were to be filed with a newly established Interstate Commerce Commission. But the Commission's hands were quickly tied by the Courts and new legislation was necessary (1906, 1910, 1913) before some control over rates was vested in the Commission.

✓   ✓   ✓

For a long time . . . the power of the Federal Government in the regulation of commerce between the States was put forth by way of negation rather than affirmatively; that is, to say, it was put forth in restraint of excessive State power when it appeared, instead of by way of affirmative national regulation. The national restraint, when there was any, was commonly effected by invoking the action of the judicial department of the Government, and by its assistance arresting such State action as appeared to constitute an unauthorized interference with interstate traffic and intercourse. This special intervention, whether in the exercise of an original jurisdiction, as in the Wheel-

[21] *First Annual Report of the Interstate Commerce Commission* (December 1, 1887), pp. 4-9.

ing Bridge case, reported in 13 Howard, 518, or under an appellate authority, as in Ward *v.* Maryland (12 Wallace, 418), and Welton *v.* Missouri (91 United States Reports, 275), has been important and useful in a considerable number of cases, but in the nature of things it could not accomplish the purposes of general regulation. On the other hand, the effect was to leave the corporations, into whose hands the internal commerce of the country had principally fallen, to make the law for themselves in many important particulars—the State power being inadequate to complete regulation, and the national power not being put forth for the purpose.

The common law still remained operative, but there were many reasons why it was inadequate for the purposes of complete regulation. One very obvious reason was that the new method of land transportation was wholly unknown to the common law, and was so different from those under which common-law rules had grown up, that doubts and differences of opinion as to the extent to which those rules could be made applicable were inevitable. A highway of which the ownership is in private citizens or corporations who permit no other vehicles but their own to run upon it bears obviously but faint resemblance to the common highway upon which every man may walk or ride or drive his wagon or his carriage. If we undertake to apply to the one the rules which have grown up in regulation of the others, there must necessarily be a considerable period in which the state of the law will, in many important particulars, be uncertain, and while that continues to be the case, those who have the power to act and who must necessarily act by rule and according to some established system, will for all practical purposes make the law, because the rule and the system will be of their establishment.

Such, to a considerable extent, has been the fact regarding the business of transporting persons and property by rail.

Those who have controlled the railroads have not only made rules for the government of their own corporate affairs, but very largely also they have determined at pleasure what should be the terms of their contract relations with others, and others have acquiesced, though oftentimes unwillingly, because they could not with confidence affirm that the law would not compel it, and a test of the question would be difficult and expensive. The carriers of the country were thus enabled to determine in great measure what rules should govern the transportation of persons and property; rules which intimately concerned the commercial, industrial, and social life of the people.

The circumstances of railroad development tended to make this indirect and abnormal law-making exceedingly unequal and oftentimes oppressive. When railroads began to be built the demand for participation in their benefits went up from every city and hamlet in the land, and the public was impatient of any obstacles to their free construction and of any doubts that might be suggested as to the substantial benefit to flow from any possible line that might be built. Under an imperative popular demand general laws were enacted in many States which enabled projectors of roads to organize at pleasure and select their own lines, and where there were no such laws the grant of a special charter was almost a matter of course, and the securities against abuse of corporate powers were little more than nominal. For a long time the promoter of a railway was looked upon as a public benefactor, and laws were passed under which municipal bodies were allowed to give public money or loan public credit in aid of his schemes on an assumption that almost any road would prove reasonably remunerative, but that in any event the indirect advantages which the public would reap must more than compensate for the expenditures.

In time it came to be perceived that these sanguine expectations were delusive. A very large proportion of all the public money invested in railroads was wholly sunk and lost. Many roads were undertaken by parties who were without capital, and who relied upon obtaining it by a sale of bonds to a credulous public. The corporation thus without capital was bankrupt from its inception, and the corporators were very likely to be mere adventurers who would employ their chartered powers in such manner as would most conduce to their personal ends.

It is striking proof of the recklessness of corporate management that 108 roads, representing a mileage of 11,066, are now in the hands of receivers, managing them under the direction of courts, whose attention is thus necessarily withdrawn from the ordinary and more appropriate duties of judicial bodies. So serious has been the evil of bringing worthless schemes into existence and making them the basis for an appropriation of public moneys or for the issue of worthless evidences of debt, that a number of the States have so amended their constitutions as to take from the legislature the power either to lend the credit of the State in aid of corporations proposing to construct railroads, or to authorize municipal bodies to render aid, either in money or credit. State legislation has at the same time been in the direction of making compulsory the actual payment of a bona fide capital before a corporation shall be at liberty to test the credulity of the public by an issue of negotiable securities.

When roads were built for which the business was inadequate, the managers were likely to seek support by entering upon competition for business which more legitimately belonged to the other roads, and which could only be obtained by offering rates so low that if long continued they must prove destructive. A competitive warfare was thus opened up in which each party endeavored to underbid the other, with little regard to prudential considerations, and freights were in a great many cases carried at a loss, in the hope that in time the power of the rival to continue the strife would be crippled and the field practically left to a victor who could then make its own terms with customers. When the competition was less extreme than this, there was still a great deal of earnest strife for business, some of which was open and with equal offerings of rates and accommodations to all, but very much of which was carried on secretly, and then the very large dealers practically made their own terms, being not only accommodated with side tracks and other special conveniences, but also given what were sometimes spoken of as wholesale rates, or perhaps secret rebates, which reduced the cost to them of transportation very greatly below what smaller dealers in the same line of business were compelled to pay. Such allowances were sufficient of themselves in very many cases to render successful competition, as against those who had them, practically impossible. . . .

These were some of the evils that made interference by

national legislation imperative. But there were others that were of no small importance. Rates when there was no competition were sometimes so high as to be oppressive, and when competition existed by lines upon which the public confidently relied to protect them against such a wrong, a consolidation was effected and the high rates perpetuated by that means. In some cases the roads, created as conveniences in transportation, were so managed in respect to business passing or destined to pass over other roads that they constituted hinderances instead of helps, to the great annoyance of travel and to the serious loss of those who intrusted their property to them. Then their rates were changed at pleasure and without public notification; their dealings to a large extent were kept from the public eye, the obligation of publicity not being recognized; and the public were therefore without the means of judging whether their charges for railroad service were reasonable and just or the contrary. . . .

These were serious evils; and they not only to some extent blunted the sense of right and wrong among the people and tended to fix an impression upon the public mind that unfair advantages in the competition of business were perfectly admissible when not criminal, but they built up or strengthened a class feeling and imbittered the relations between those who for every reason of interest ought to be in harmony. It was high time that adequate power should be put forth to bring them to an end. Railroads are a public agency. The authority to construct them with extraordinary privileges in management and operation is an expression of sovereign power, only given from a consideration of great public benefits which might be expected to result therefrom. From every grant of such a privilege resulted a duty of protection and regulation, that the grant might not be abused and the public defrauded of the anticipated benefits.

The abuses of corporate authority to the injury of the public were not the only reasons operating upon the public mind to bring about the legislation now under consideration; some other things which in their direct effects were wrongs to stockholders only had their influence also, and this by no means a light one. The manner in which corporate stocks were manipulated for the benefit of managers and to the destruction of the interest of the owners was often a great scandal, resulting sometimes in the bankruptcy and practical destruction of roads which, if properly managed, would have been not only profitable but widely useful. This in its direct results might be a wrong to individuals only, but in its indirect influence it was a great public wrong also.

The most striking and obvious fact in such a case commonly is that persons having control of railroads have in a very short time by means of the control amassed great fortunes. The natural conclusion which one draws who must judge from surface appearances is, that these fortunes are unfairly acquired at the expense of the public; that they represent excessive charges on railroad business, or unfair employment of inside privileges, and furnish in themselves conclusive evidence that current rates are wrong and probably extortionate. An impression of this sort, when it happens to be wide of the fact is for many reasons unfortunate. It creates or strengthens a prejudice against all railroad management—the honest as well as the dishonest—which affects the public view of all railroad questions; it renders it more difficult to deal with such questions calmly and dispassionately; it makes the public restive under the charges they are subjected to, even though they be moderate and necessary; it tends to strengthen a feeling among the unthinking that capital represents extortion. However careful, considerate, fair, and just the management of any particular road may be, and however closely it may confine itself to its legitimate business, it is impossible that it should wholly escape the ill effects of this prejudice, which are visited upon all roads because some conspicuous railroad managers have by their misconduct given in the public mind a character to all.

Evils of the class last mentioned were difficult of legislative correction, because they sprang from the over-confidence of stockholders in the officers chosen to manage their interests, and whose acts at the time they perhaps assented to. But if capable of correction by any legislative authority, it was in general that of the States, not that of the nation. The States in the main conferred the corporate power, and it was for the States by their legislation to provide for the protection of the individual interests which were brought into existence by their permission. The National Government had to do with the commerce which these artificial entities of State creation might be concerned in. Nevertheless, the manifest misuse of corporate powers strengthened the demand for national legislation, and this very naturally, because the private gains resulting from corporate abuse were supposed to spring, to some extent at least, from excessive burdens imposed upon the commerce which the nation ought to regulate and protect.

For the purpose of correcting the evils above alluded to, so far as it was constitutionally competent for national legislation to do so, the act to regulate commerce lays down certain rules to be observed by the carriers to which its provisions apply, which are intended to be and emphatically are rules of equity and equality and which, if properly observed, ought to and in time will restore the management of the transportation business of the country to public confidence.

23

THE SHERMAN ANTITRUST ACT OF JULY 2, 1890[22]

The concern over the appearance of large industrial combinations led to the establishment of the Interstate Commerce Act in 1887 and the passage of the Sherman Antitrust Act in 1890. Neither law initially was effective and both had to be strengthened. It should be noted, however, that antitrust legislation in America at least has afforded a device by which the practices of large business can be scrutinized and imperfect competition in a measure kept under control. To this extent the antitrust laws of the United States have kept monopoly in check more so than any other industrial country in the world.

↑   ↑   ↑

—An act to protect trade and commerce against unlawful restraints and monopolies.

Be it enacted by the Senate and House of Representatives of the United States of America in Congress assembled,

SEC. 1. Every contract, combination in the form of trust or otherwise, or conspiracy, in restraint of trade or commerce among the several States, or with foreign nations, is hereby declared to be illegal. Every person who shall make any such contract or engage in any such combination or conspiracy, shall be deemed guilty of a misdemeanor, and, on conviction thereof, shall be punished by fine not exceeding five thousand dollars, or by imprisonment not

[22] *U. S. Statutes at Large,* Vol. 26, 51st Congress, 1st Session, Ch. 647, pp. 209-210.

exceeding one year, or by both said punishments, in the discretion of the court.

SEC. 2. Every person who shall monopolize, or attempt to monopolize, or combine or conspire with any other person or persons, to monopolize any part of the trade or commerce among the several States, or with foreign nations, shall be deemed guilty of a misdemeanor, and, on conviction thereof, shall be punished by fine not exceeding five thousand dollars, or by imprisonment not exceeding one year, or by both said punishments, in the discretion of the court.

SEC. 3. Every contract, combination in form of trust or otherwise,, or conspiracy, in restraint of trade or commerce in any Territory of the United States or of the District of Columbia, or in restraint of trade or commerce between any such Territory and another, or between any such Territory or Territories and any State or States or the District of Columbia, or with foreign nations, or between the District of Columbia and any State or States or foreign nations, is hereby declared illegal. Every person who shall make any such contract or engage in any such combination or conspiracy, shall be deemed guilty of a misdemeanor, and, on conviction thereof, shall be punished by fine not exceeding five thousand dollars, or by imprisonment not exceeding one year, or by both said punishments, in the discretion of the court.

SEC. 4. The several circuit courts of the United States are hereby invested with jurisdiction to prevent and restrain violations of this act; and it shall be the duty of the several district attorneys of the United States, in their respective districts, under the direction of the Attorney-General, to institute proceedings in equity to prevent and restrain such violations. Such proceedings may be by way of petition setting forth the case and praying that such violation shall be enjoined or otherwise prohibited. When the parties complained of shall have been duly notified of such petition the court shall proceed, as soon as may be, to the hearing and determination of the case; and pending such petition and before final decree, the court may at any time make such temporary restraining order or prohibition as shall be deemed just in the premises.

SEC. 5. Whenever it shall appear to the court before

which any proceeding under section four of this act may be pending, that the ends of justice require that other parties should be brought before the court, the court may cause them to be summoned, whether they reside in the district in which the court is held or not; and subpœnas to that end may be served in any district by the marshal thereof.

SEC. 6. Any property owned under any contract or by any combination, or pursuant to any conspiracy (and being the subject thereof) mentioned in section one of this act, and being in the course of transportation from one State to another, or to a foreign country, shall be forfeited to the United States, and may be seized and condemned by like proceedings as those provided by law for the forfeiture, seizure, and condemnation of property imported into the United States contrary to law.

SEC. 7. Any person who shall be injured in his business or property by any other person or corporation by reason of anything forbidden or declared to be unlawful by this act, may sue therefor in any circuit court of the United States in the district in which the defendant resides or is found, without respect to the amount in controversy, and shall recover three fold the damages by him sustained, and the costs of suit, including a reasonable attorney's fee.

SEC. 8. That the word "person," or "persons," wherever used in this act shall be deemed to include corporations and associations existing under or authorized by the laws of either the United States, the laws of any of the Territories, the laws of any State, or the laws of any foreign country.

— 24 —

THE SHERMAN SILVER PURCHASE ACT OF JULY 14, 1890[23]

As a result of the clamor of the easy-money people and the silver interests—for silver once more began to be mined, and the Coinage Act of 1873 had virtually demonetized silver—Congress passed the Bland-Allison Silver Purchase Act of 1878 which, however, not only limited the purchase of silver but also limited the use of silver certificates that were issued. These shortcomings were rectified by the Silver Act of 1890, which made it possible for the Treasury to purchase all the silver mined and at the same time issue against these purchases Treasury notes of full legal tender. In 1878, the silver-gold ratio stood at 18 to 1; in 1890, at 20 to 1. Under the Bland-Allison Act, 1878-1890, 378 million dollars in silver were minted; under the Sherman Act, 1890-93, the total was $153 million. The Sherman Act was repealed in 1893.

✦   ✦   ✦

—An act directing the purchase of silver bullion and the issue of Treasury notes thereon, and for other purposes.

Be it enacted by the Senate and House of Representatives of the United States of America in Congress assembled, That the Secretary of the Treasury is hereby directed to purchase, from time to time, silver bullion to the aggregate amount of four million five hundred thousand ounces, or so much thereof as may be offered in each month, at the market price thereof, not exceeding one dollar for three hundred and seventy-one and twenty-five

[23] *U. S. Statutes at Large,* Vol. 26, 51st Congress, 1st Session, Ch. 708, p. 289.

hundredths grains of pure silver, and to issue in payment for such purchases of silver bullion Treasury notes of the United States to be prepared by the Secretary of the Treasury, in such form and of such denominations, not less than one dollar nor more than one thousand dollars, as he may prescribe, and a sum sufficient to carry into effect the provisions of this act is hereby appropriated out of any money in the Treasury not otherwise appropriated.

SEC. 2. That the Treasury notes issued in accordance with the provisions of this act shall be redeemable on demand, in coin, at the Treasury of the United States, or at the office of any assistant treasurer of the United States, and when so redeemed may be reissued; but no greater or less amount of such notes shall be outstanding at any time than the cost of the silver bullion and the standard silver dollars coined therefrom, then held in the Treasury purchased by such notes; and such Treasury notes shall be a legal tender in payment of all debts, public and private, except where otherwise expressly stipulated in the contract, and shall be receivable for customs, taxes, and all public dues, and when so received may be reissued; and such notes, when held by any national banking association, may be counted as a part of its lawful reserve. That upon demand of the holder of any of the Treasury notes herein provided for the Secretary of the Treasury shall, under such regulations as he may prescribe, redeem such notes in gold or silver coin, at his discretion, it being the established policy of the United States to maintain the two metals on a parity with each other upon the present legal ratio, or such ratio as may be provided by law.

SEC. 3. That the Secretary of the Treasury shall each month coin two million ounces of the silver bullion purchased under the provisions of this act into standard silver dollars until the first day of July eighteen hundred and ninety-one, and after that time he shall coin of the silver bullion purchased under the provisions of this act as much as may be necessary to provide for the redemption of the Treasury notes herein provided for, and any gain or seigniorage arising from such coinage shall be accounted for and paid into the Treasury. . . .

SEC. 5. That so much of the act of February twenty-eighth, eighteen hundred and seventy-eight, entitled "An act to authorize the coinage of the standard silver dollar and to restore its legal-tender character," as requires the monthly purchase and coinage of the same into silver dollars of not less than two million dollars, nor more than four million dollars' worth of silver bullion, is hereby repealed. . . .

THE PEOPLE'S PARTY PLATFORM AT OMAHA, JULY 3, 1892 [24]

The complaints against speculative, corporate, and alien land ownership came to a head in the Populist platform of 1892, written by Ignatius Donnelly. This was an amazing document of discontent, striking out in all those directions where the farmers thought they saw their oppressors mobilized and functioning. An interesting proposal included was the so-called Sub-Treasury plan of the Farmers' Alliance, a device for extending farm credit on the basis of the storage of surplus crops. It was not until the New Deal's agricultural programs were enacted, in the 1930's, that this idea—much ridiculed by the economists of the 1890's—became one of the important props of farm support.

The conditions which surround us best justify our cooperation. We meet in the midst of a nation brought to the verge of moral, political and material ruin. Corruption dominates the ballot box, the Legislatures, the Congress, and touches even the ermine of the Bench. The people are demoralized; most of the States have been compelled to isolate the voters at the polling places to prevent universal intimidation or bribery. The newspapers are largely subsidized or muzzled, public opinion silenced, business prostrated, our homes covered with mortgages, labor impoverished, and the land concentrating in the hands of the capitalists. The urban workmen are denied the right of organization for self-protection; imported pauperized labor beats down their wages; a hireling standing army, unrecognized by our laws, is established to shoot them down,

[24] *McPherson's Handbook of Politics for 1892*, pp. 269-270.

and they are rapidly degenerating into European conditions. The fruits of the toil of millions are boldly stolen to build up colossal fortunes for a few, unprecedented in the history of mankind, and the possessors of these in turn despise the Republic and endanger liberty. From the same prolific womb of governmental injustice we breed the two great classes—tramps and millionaires.

The national power to create money is appropriated to enrich bond-holders; a vast public debt, payable in legal tender currency, has been funded into gold-bearing bonds, thereby adding millions to the burdens of the people.

Silver, which has been accepted as coin since the dawn of history, has been demonetized to add to the purchasing power of gold by decreasing the value of all forms of property as well as human labor, and the supply of currency is purposely abridged to fatten usurers, bankrupt enterprise and enslave industry.

A vast conspiracy against mankind has been organized on two continents, and it is rapidly taking possession of the world. If not met and overthrown at once, it forebodes terrible social convulsions, the destruction of civilization, or the establishment of an absolute despotism.

We have witnessed, for more than a quarter of a century, the struggles of the two great political parties for power and plunder, while grievous wrongs have been inflicted upon the suffering people. We charge that the controlling influences dominating both these parties have permitted the existing dreadful conditions to develop without serious effort to prevent or restrain them.

OLD PARTIES TREATED AS ONE

Neither do they now promise us any substantial reform. They have agreed together to ignore, in the coming campaign, every issue but one. They propose to drown the outcries of a plundered people with the uproar of a sham battle over the tariff, so that capitalists, corporations, national banks, rings, trusts, watered stock, the demonetization of silver and the oppressions of the usurers may all be lost sight of. They propose to sacrifice our homes, lives and children, on the altar of mammon; to destroy the multitude in order to secure corruption funds from the millionaires.

Assembled on the anniversary of the birthday of the nation, and filled with the spirit of the grand general and chieftain who established our independence, we seek to restore the Government of the Republic to the hands of the "plain people" with whose class it originated. We assert our purposes to be identical with the purposes of the National Constitution, to form a more perfect Union and establish justice, insure domestic tranquility, provide for the common defense, promote the general welfare and secure the blessings of liberty for ourselves and our posterity.

We declare that this Republic can only endure as a free government while built upon the love of the whole people for each other and for the nation; that it cannot be pinned together by bayonets; that the civil war is over and that every passion and resentment which grew out of it must die with it, and that we must be in fact, as we are in name, one united brotherhood of freedom.

FARMERS' DEMANDS

Our country finds itself confronted by conditions for which there is no precedent in the history of the world; our annual agricultural productions amount to billions of dollars in value, which must within a few weeks or months be exchanged for billions of dollars' worth of commodities consumed in their production; the existing currency supply is wholly inadequate to make this exchange; the results are falling prices, the formation of combines and rings, the impoverishment of the producing class. We pledge ourselves that, if given power, we will labor to correct these evils by wise and reasonable legislation, in accordance with the terms of our platform.

We believe that the powers of government—in other words, of the people—should be expanded (as in the case of the postal service) as rapidly and as far as the good sense of an intelligent people and the teachings of experience shall justify, to the end that oppression, injustice and poverty, shall eventually cease in the land.

While our sympathies as a party of reform are naturally upon the side of every proposition which will tend to make men intelligent, virtuous and temperate, we nevertheless regard these questions—important as they are—as secondary to the great issues now pressing for solution, and upon which not only our individual prosperity, but the very existence of free institutions depend; and we ask all men to first help us to determine whether we are to have a Republic to administer, before we differ as to the conditions upon which it is to be administered; believing that the forces of reform this day organized will never cease to move forward, until every wrong is righted, and equal rights and equal privileges securely established for all the men and women of this country. We declare, therefore,

PERPETUAL LABOR UNION

First—That the union of the labor forces of the United States this day consummated shall be permanent and perpetual; may its spirit enter into all hearts for the salvation of the Republic, and the uplifting of mankind.

WEALTH FOR WORKERS

Second—Wealth belongs to him who creates it, and every dollar taken from industry without an equivalent is robbery. "If any will not work, neither shall he eat." The interests of rural and civic labor are the same; their enemies are identical.

OWNERSHIP OF RAILWAYS

Third—We believe that the time has come when the railroad corporations will either own the people or the people must own the railroads; and should the Government enter upon the work of owning and managing all railroads, we should favor an amendment to the Constitution by which all persons engaged in the Government service shall be placed under a civil service regulation of the most rigid character, so as to prevent the increase of the power of the national administration by the use of such additional Government employes.

FINANCE

1st. We demand a national currency, safe, sound and flexible, issued by the General Government only, a full legal tender for all debts public and private, and that without the use of banking corporations; a just, equitable and efficient means of distribution direct to the people at a tax not to exceed 2 per cent. per annum, to be provided as set forth in the Sub-Treasury plan of the Farmers' Alliance, or a better system; also by payments in discharge of its obligations for public inprovements.

(A) We demand free and unlimited coinage of silver and gold at the present legal ratio of 16 to 1.

(B) We demand that the amount of circulating medium be speedily increased to not less than $50 per capita.

(C) We demand a graduated income tax.

(D) We believe that the money of the country should be kept as much as possible in the hands of the people, and hence we demand that all State and National revenues shall be limited to the necessary expenses of the Government, economically and honestly administered.

(E) We demand that Postal Savings Banks be established by the Government for the safe deposit of the earnings of the people and to facilitate exchange.

TRANSPORTATION

2d. Transportation being a means of exchange and a public necessity, the government should own and operate the railroads in the interest of the people.

The telegraph and telephone, like the post office system, being a necessity for the transmission of news, should be owned and operated by the Government in the interest of the people.

LAND

3d. The land, including all the natural sources of wealth, is the heritage of the people and should not be monopolized for speculative purposes, and alien ownership of land should be prohibited. All land now held by railroads and other corporations in excess of their actual needs, and all lands now owned by aliens, should be reclaimed by the Government and held for actual settlers only. . . .

— 26 —

CLEVELAND ON THE REPEAL OF THE SHERMAN SILVER PURCHASE ACT, AUGUST 8, 1893 [25]

President Cleveland, caught in the depression beginning in 1893, regarded the Silver Purchase Act of 1893—because it contributed to the drain upon the Treasury's gold —as the source of all of the country's difficulties. He called upon Congress to authorize the Treasury to stop purchasing silver; it acceded to his request; but gold continued to flow out of the Treasury and the country. The fact is—as we know today—that tinkering with the money supply, and, in fact, reducing it, was not calculated to help the country avoid the hardships of mass disemployment and wholesale commercial failures. The depression had to spend its course, by 1897, before recovery once more set in.

The existence of an alarming and extraordinary situation involving the welfare and prosperity of all our people has constrained me to call together in extra session the people's representatives in Congress, to the end that through a wise and patriotic exercise of the legislative duty with which they solely are charged, present evils may be mitigated and dangers threatening the future may be averted.

[25] Richardson, James, ed., *Messages and Papers of the Presidents*, Vol. 9, pp. 401-405.

Our unfortunate financial plight is not the result of untoward events nor of conditions related to our natural resources, nor is it traceable to any of the afflictions which frequently check national growth and prosperity. With plenteous crops, with abundant promise of remunerative production and manufacture, with unusual invitation to safe investment, and with satisfactory assurance to business enterprise, suddenly financial distrust and fear have sprung up on every side. Numerous moneyed institutions have suspended because abundant assets were not immediately available to meet the demands of frightened depositors. Surviving corporations and individuals are content to keep in hand the money they are usually anxious to loan, and those engaged in legitimate business are surprised to find that the securities they offer for loans, though heretofore satisfactory, are no longer accepted. Values supposed to be fixed are fast becoming conjectural, and loss and failure have invaded every branch of business.

I believe these things are principally chargeable to Congressional legislation touching the purchase and coinage of silver by the General Government.

This legislation is embodied in a statute passed on the 14th day of July, 1890, which was the culmination of much agitation on the subject involved, and which may be considered a truce, after a long struggle, between the advocates of free silver coinage and those intending to be more conservative.

Undoubtedly the monthly purchases by the Government of 4,500,000 ounces of silver, enforced under that statute, were regarded by those interested in silver production as a certain guaranty of its increase in price. The result, however, has been entirely different, for immediately following a spasmodic and slight rise the price of silver began to fall after the passage of the act, and has since reached the lowest point ever known. This disappointing result has led to renewed and persistent effort in the direction of free silver coinage.

Meanwhile not only are the evil effects of the operation of the present law constantly accumulating, but the result to which its execution must inevitably lead is becoming palpable to all who give the least heed to financial subjects.

This law provides that in payment for the 4,500,000

ounces of silver bullion which the Secretary of the Treasury is commanded to purchase monthly there shall be issued Treasury notes redeemable on demand in gold or silver coin, at the discretion of the Secretary of the Treasury, and that said notes may be reissued. It is, however, declared in the act to be "the established policy of the United States to maintain the two metals on a parity with each other upon the present legal ratio or such ratio as may be provided by law." This declaration so controls the action of the Secretary of the Treasury as to prevent his exercising the discretion nominally vested in him if by such action the parity between gold and silver may be disturbed. Manifestly a refusal by the Secretary to pay these Treasury notes in gold if demanded would necessarily result in their discredit and depreciation as obligations payable only in silver, and would destroy the parity between the two metals by establishing a discrimination in favor of gold.

Up to the 15th day of July, 1893, these notes had been issued in payment of silver-bullion purchases to the amount of more than $147,000,000. While all but a very small quantity of this bullion remains uncoined and without usefulness in the Treasury, many of the notes given in its purchase have been paid in gold. This is illustrated by the statement that between the 1st day of May, 1892, and the 15th day of July, 1893, the notes of this kind issued in payment for silver bullion amounted to a little more than $54,000,000, and that during the same period about $49,000,000 were paid by the Treasury in gold for the redemption of such notes.

The policy necessarily adopted of paying these notes in gold has not spared the gold reserve of $100,000,000 long ago set aside by the Government for the redemption of other notes, for this fund has already been subjected to the payment of new obligations amounting to about $150,000,000 on account of silver purchases, and has as a consequence for the first time since its creation been encroached upon.

We have thus made the depletion of our gold easy and have tempted other and more appreciative nations to add it to their stock. That the opportunity we have offered has not been neglected is shown by the large amounts of gold which have been recently drawn from our Treasury and exported to increase the financial strength of foreign nations. The excess of exports of gold over its imports for the year ending June 30, 1893, amounted to more than $87,500,000.

Between the 1st day of July, 1890, and the 15th day of July, 1893, the gold coin and bullion in our Treasury decreased more than $132,000,000, while during the same period the silver coin and bullion in the Treasury increased more than $147,000,000. Unless Government bonds are to be constantly issued and sold to replenish our exhausted gold, only to be again exhausted, it is apparent that the operation of the silver-purchase law now in force leads in the direction of the entire substitution of silver for the gold in the Government Treasury, and that this must be followed by the payment of all Government obligations in depreciated silver.

At this stage gold and silver must part company and the Government must fail in its established policy to maintain the two metals on a parity with each other. Given over to the exclusive use of a currency greatly depreciated according to the standard of the commercial world, we could no longer claim a place among nations of the first class, nor could our Government claim a performance of its obligation, so far as such an obligation has been imposed upon it, to provide for the use of the people the best and safest money.

If, as many of its friends claim, silver ought to occupy a larger place in our currency and the currency of the world through general international cooperation and agreement, it is obvious that the United States will not be in a position to gain a hearing in favor of such an arrangement so long as we are willing to continue our attempt to accomplish the result single-handed.

The knowledge in business circles among our own people that our Government can not make its fiat equivalent to intrinsic value nor keep inferior money on a parity with superior money by its own independent efforts has resulted in such a lack of confidence at home in the stability of currency values that capital refuses its aid to new enterprises, while millions are actually withdrawn from the channels of trade and commerce to become idle and unproductive in the hands of timid owners. Foreign investors, equally alert, not only decline to purchase American securities, but make haste to sacrifice those which they already have.

It does not meet the situation to say that apprehension in regard to the future of our finances is groundless and that there is no reason for lack of confidence in the purposes or power of the Government in the premises. The very existence of this apprehension and lack of confidence, however caused, is a menace which ought not for a moment to be disregarded. Possibly, if the undertaking we have in hand were the maintenance of a specific known quantity of silver at a parity with gold, our ability to do so might be estimated and gauged, and perhaps, in view of our unparalleled growth and resources, might be favorably passed upon. But when our avowed endeavor is to maintain such parity in regard to an amount of silver increasing at the rate of $50,000,000 yearly, with no fixed termination to such increase, it can hardly be said that a problem is presented whose solution is free from doubt.

The people of the United States are entitled to a sound and stable currency and to money recognized as such on every exchange and in every market of the world. Their Government has no right to injure them by financial experiments opposed to the policy and practice of other civilized states, nor is it justified in permitting an exaggerated and unreasonable reliance on our national strength and ability to jeopardize the soundness of the people's money.

This matter rises above the plane of party politics. It vitally concerns every business and calling and enters every household in the land. There is one important aspect of the subject which especially should never be overlooked. At times like the present, when the evils of unsound finance threaten us, the speculator may anticipate a harvest gathered from the misfortune of others, the capitalist may protect himself by hoarding or may even find profit in the fluctuations of values; but the wage earner—the first to be injured by a depreciated currency and the last to receive the benefit of its correction—is practically defenseless. He relies for work upon the ventures of confident and contented capital. This failing him, his condition is without alleviation, for he can neither prey on the misfortunes of others nor hoard his labor. One of the greatest statesmen our country has known, speaking more than fifty years ago, when a derangement of the currency had ceased commercial distress, said:

The very man of all others who has the deepest interest in a sound currency and who suffers most by mischievous legislation in money matters is the man who earns his daily bread by his daily toil.

These words are as pertinent now as on the day they were uttered, and ought to impressively remind us that a failure in the discharge of our duty at this time must especially injure those of our countrymen who labor, and who because of their number and condition are entitled to the most watchful care of their Government.

It is of the utmost importance that such relief as Congress can afford in the existing situation be afforded at once. The maxim "He gives twice who gives quickly" is directly applicable. It may be true that the embarrassments from which the business of the country is suffering arise as much from evils apprehended as from those actually existing. We may hope, too, that calm counsels will prevail, and that neither the capitalists nor the wage earners will give way to unreasoning panic and sacrifice their property or their interests under the influence of exaggerated fears. Nevertheless, every day's delay in removing one of the plain and principal causes of the present state of things enlarges the mischief already done and increases the responsibility of the Government for its existence. Whatever else the people have a right to expect from Congress, they may certainly demand that legislation condemned by the ordeal of three years' disastrous experience shall be removed from the statute books as soon as their representatives can legitimately deal with it.

It was my purpose to summon Congress in special session early in the coming September, that we might enter promptly upon the work of tariff reform, which the true interests of the country clearly demand, which so large a majority of the people, as shown by their suffrages, desire and expect, and to the accomplishment of which every effort of the present Administration is pledged. But while tariff reform has lost nothing of its immediate and permanent importance and must in the near future engage the attention of Congress, it has seemed to me that the financial condition of the country should at once and before all other subjects be considered by your honorable body.

I earnestly recommend the prompt repeal of the provisions of the act passed July 14, 1890, authorizing the purchase of silver bullion, and that other legislative action may put beyond all doubt or mistake the intention and the ability of the Government to fulfill its pecuniary obligations in money universally recognized by all civilized countries.

RESUMPTION OF FEDERAL HIGHWAY CONSTRUCTION, 1893-1916 [26]

Not until 1893 was the Federal government prepared to embark once more on road construction; and by 1916 it was committed to a fully coordinated plan based on Federal aid and State control and maintenance.

✓   ✓   ✓

The consummation that is the desire of everyone is a connected system of highways which will permit the free flow of travel from point to point without the annoyance of frequent interruptions by unimproved roads. We began moving toward that end in 1891, when New Jersey passed its State-aid law. The movement was accelerated and the ultimate attainment of the end was assured when, on July 11, 1916, the President signed the Federal-aid road act.

A hundred years before the Federal Government had been active in the construction of roads. Many of the principal roads of the West and Middle West were originally laid out and built as military roads connecting the forts which dotted what was then a wild and sparsely settled country. In 1811 it began the construction of the great National Pike, which was to extend from Cumberland, Md., to St. Louis, on the Mississippi, and serve as one of the principal arteries of communication for the settlement of the great Northwest Territory. The improvement of this road was carried on more or less actively until 1840, and the road was built and surfaced with stone

---

[26] Department of Agriculture, *Yearbook* (1924), pp. 101-103.

throughout practically the entire distance from Cumberland to the western Indiana line, when it became apparent that the newly constructed railways would rapidly replace the highways as the ties which would unite the far-flung settlements that were springing up over a vast area. So strong was the conviction that the highway would be practically entirely displaced by the new kind of transportation that the National Pike for the rest of its length, from the Indiana line across Illinois to St. Louis, was not surfaced with stone, but was graded, in the belief that the grade would eventually serve a railroad. The last Federal appropriation for the National Pike or Cumberland Road, as it was called, was made in 1838. From that time until 1893 the National Government took no part whatever in the construction and maintenance of the roads.

In that year there was created in the Department of Agriculture a small office with an annual appropriation of $10,000, which was assigned the task of studying the existing highway situation and reporting upon the best methods of road construction and maintenance. This Office of Road Inquiry, as it was called, was destined to continue its work of study and research from year to year, imparting to the local road builders the knowledge it gained by building as models short sections of road, known as object-lesson roads, in numerous counties.

When, finally, in 1916 the passage of the Federal-aid road act provided for resumption of active Federal participation in road construction the former Office of Road Inquiry, then grown into the Bureau of Public Roads, was given the duty of supervising for the Government the construction of the Federal-aid roads, and its long study of road conditions throughout the country enabled it to perform that duty with intelligence and efficiency.

To the extent of the money it appropriated, the Federal-aid road act authorized the Secretary of Agriculture to participate in the improvement of post roads up to 50 per cent of the cost of the improvement, providing that the aid granted to any particular project did not exceed $10,000 a mile, exclusive of the cost of bridges more than 20 feet long. But the most important and far-reaching provision of the law was its requirement that the States desiring to receive the Federal aid would first have to create a State highway department adequate in authority and equipment to cooperate with the Federal Government and assume the responsibility for the immediate supervision of the construction. Up to the year before its passage there were still six States which had no State highway department, and a number of the departments that had been created had been given only nominal authority. As the wisdom of the policy of State control had been thoroughly proved through a score of years, the Federal act made its adoption a condition of the receipt of the Federal aid and thus at one stroke brought about the creation of departments in the laggard States and made State control a real factor in highway construction in a number in which it had hitherto been only nominal. The first Federal act, therefore, had the effect of accelerating a tendency toward State control which had already been proved to be the wisest course by the experience of the leading States.

Upon the foundation thus laid down the Federal highway act, passed five years later, added two other requirements which are destined to have a profound effect upon the course of highway improvement. First, it authorized the Secretary of Agriculture, in cooperation with the State highway departments, to designate a system of main interstate and intercounty highways, limited in each State to 7 per cent of the total mileage existing at the time of its passage, and thus imposed upon the backward States another important principle which had previously been found successful in the experience of the leading States. The act of 1916 having brought about the universal adoption of the principle of State control of main roads, this new act led to the adoption of a definite program of improvement, extensive enough to serve the most imperative needs of all States and the Nation as a whole, but so limited that its completion can be expected in a few years. And to this requirement it added the further stipulation that the roads built must be maintained—by the State highway departments if, as is confidently expected, they will, but if not, then by the Federal Government.

The importance of the Federal legislation then is that it embodies and applies those principles which have been found to be most successful in the experience of the most advanced States, and it has caused the adoption of these principles by all States much sooner than they would have been adopted on the initiative of the States. Among these principles, the application of which is extended to all States by the Federal laws, are (1) the engineering control of main roads by State highway departments, (2) the designation of connected systems of main roads to be constructed under state supervision with funds under state control and (3) the continuous maintenance of such roads by the State highway departments. . . .

In accordance with the Federal highway Act, the Secretary of Agriculture, acting through the Bureau of Public Roads and the official State highway departments, has recently designated the roads which constitute the Federal-aid highway system. These roads, which form a connected system covering the entire United States, have at present a total length of 171,687 miles. The greatest mileage which can be included in the system under the terms of the act, is approximately 200,000 miles. The roads, thus officially designated . . . reach directly nearly every city of 5,000 population or greater, and are so chosen that if a zone 10 miles wide was marked off on each side of them, these zones would include the homes of 90 per cent of the population.

MANUFACTURING ADVANTAGES OF THE UNITED STATES, 1900[27]

From time to time the Census Bureau engaged in speculation, as it did when it viewed the impressive industrial growth of the United States at the turn of the twentieth century. Here is an interesting statement of some of the reasons for America's becoming the leading manufacturing nation of the world.

✓ ✓ ✓

This rapid rise of the United States to the first position among manufacturing nations is attributable to certain distinct causes, natural and otherwise, five of which may be definitely formulated as follows:

1. Agricultural resources.
2. Mineral resources.
3. Highly developed transportation facilities.
4. Freedom of trade between states and territories.
5. Freedom from inherited and over-conservative ideas.

A study of these causes affords an explanation of the great development of manufacturing in the United States in the past, as well as an indication of its possibilities in the future.

1. *Agricultural Resources.*—Most obvious among the natural advantages of the United States is its possession of every variety of soil, and every climate, except the tropical. There is thus an abundance of food supplies of almost every form for the consumption of the people, and abundant raw agricultural materials for the use of manu-

[27] Twelfth Census of the U. S. *Reports,* Vol. 7, Pt. I, *U. S. by Industries* (Washington, 1902), pp. LVI-LIX.

factures. Both food supplies and agricultural materials for manufacture are cheaper, more abundant, and more varied in the United States than in any other manufacturing country. As a consequence, the manufacturing development of the country has extended to nearly every form of industry which ministers to the comfort and necessities of man. In many localities the character of the manufactures has been determined largely by climatic conditions and by the character of products to which the soil of such localities is especially adapted.

In the production of cotton, the leading textile staple, the United States is preeminent, furnishing 86.1 per cent of the world's production of cotton in 1899-1900. . . .

The forests of the United States furnish practically all the material required for the extensive wood-working industries of the country, and lumber valued at more than $30,000,000 is now exported annually. The only foreign sources upon which the United States relies for additional supplies of lumber are Canada, the West Indies, and Central and South America, the last two furnishing mahogany, rosewood, Spanish cedar, etc., required in the manufacture of pianos and fine furniture.

2. *Mineral Resources.*—In the second place, the United States produces nearly every mineral required for manufacturing industries. In most of these the supplies appear to be sufficient for years to come, and are obtainable at prices which compare favorably with prices in other parts of the world.

Coal, the basis of modern manufactures, exists in great abundance, and the fields are so widely distributed throughout the country as to afford easy transportation, by rail or water, to the chief distributing points and manufacturing centers. The total production of coal in the United States in 1899 was 175,428,300 metric tons of bituminous coal, valued at $167,935,304, and 54,825,776 metric tons of anthracite coal, valued at $88,142,130. Reference should be made also to the extensive supplies of natural gas, a fuel which is utilized chiefly in manufacturing. In 1899 the estimated value of natural gas was $20,024,873. It is impossible to ascertain from the census reports the actual consumption of coal in manufacturing, but the reported cost of all fuel consumed in manufacturing during the

census year was $205,320,632. The coal production of the
United States is now larger than that of any other country,
having passed the production of Great Britain for the first
time in 1899. . . .

A supply of iron ore is equally important to the manufacturing development of a country. Table VII shows that
in this mineral, as in production of coal, the United States
leads all countries.

. . . The production of iron ore in the United States
increased 53.9 per cent between 1890 and 1899, constituting
28.5 per cent of the world's estimated production in 1890
and 31.8 per cent in 1899. The stimulus these supplies of
the ore have given to the manufacture of iron is seen in the
remarkable advance in this industry during the last two
decades. The United States passed Great Britain between
1880 and 1890, becoming the leading pig-iron producing
country in the world. Between 1890 and 1899 the increase
in production in the United States was 4,418,000 tons,
while in Great Britain it was 1,401,105 tons. The pig-iron
production of the United States in 1899 was 13,620,703
tons, or 34.1 per cent of the world's production.

A special advantage connected with the abundance of
coal and iron ores in the United States is the fact that
deposits of these minerals, together with deposits of lime-
stone, which is used for fluxing the iron ore, are frequently
found in the same locality, thus greatly facilitating their
use in manufactures.

In the production of crude copper the advance of the
United States to the front rank has been even more rapid
and remarkable. Statistics of the world's output in 1850
place the copper production of all countries in that year at
52,250 tons, to which quantity Chile contributed 14,300
tons, Great Britain, 11,800 tons, Russia, 6,000 tons, Japan,
3,000 tons, and the United States only 650 tons. In 1899
the world's output of copper was estimated at 463,303
long tons, of which quantity the United States produced
253,870 long tons, or nearly four hundred times its production in 1850. The production in 1899 constituted 54.8
per cent of the world's estimated production, . . . placing
the United States first in this field also. . . .

There is also an abundance of most of the minor metals.
The production of lead increased from 143,630 short tons

in 1890 to 210,500 short tons in 1899; zinc production increased from 63,683 short tons in 1890 to 129,051 short tons in 1899; quicksilver from 22,926 flasks (of 76½ pounds avoirdupois net) in 1890 to 30,454 flasks in 1899; and aluminum from 61,281 pounds (including aluminum alloys) in 1890 to 5,200,000 pounds in 1899. There have been corresponding increases in the production of practically all the nonmetallic minerals consumed in manufactures.

On the other hand, the United States relies in constantly decreasing degree upon the ores of other countries. Where these are imported it is chiefly in the form of pigs and bars. The principal imports of this character for consumption during the fiscal year 1899, were 67,362,207 pounds of tin in bars, blocks, pigs, etc., valued at $11,843,357; 9,237,064 pounds of lead-bearing ores of all kinds valued at $185,872; 4,760.5 pounds of platinum in ingots, bars, etc., valued at $951,154; 21,028 tons of nickel ore and matte, valued at $1,183,924; and 48,017 tons of copper ores, valued at $608,399.

3. *Transportation Facilities.*—Another important advantage possessed by manufacturers in the United States is the unusual facilities for transportation, particularly in the more thickly settled sections, where manufacturing industries predominate. Over 18,000 miles of navigable rivers not only facilitate transportation directly but cause competition with railroads, and thus make possible the cheap marketing of products. The coastwise trade of the United States exceeds that of any other country. It includes steamship lines to and from New York, Boston, Philadelphia, Baltimore, and other points, and between several of these cities and Charleston, Richmond, Savannah, Jacksonville, New Orleans, Galveston, and other Southern ports.

In recent years navigation on the great lakes has become a most important factor in the internal traffic of the country. These lakes, with the Sault Ste. Marie and Canadian canals around the rapids of the St. Marys river, the St. Clair river, the Detroit river, and the Welland canal, allow unbroken navigation between Duluth and the eastern end of Lake Ontario, a distance of 1,000 miles.

The development of freight traffic over this route has been so great during the past decade, that in 1899 it had become the greatest internal waterway in the world, having a ton mileage equal to nearly 40 per cent of that of the entire railroad system of the United States. In 1899 more than five times as many vessels passed through the United States and Canadian canals at Sault Ste. Marie as through the Suez canal. . . .

The railroad systems of the United States were constructed with great rapidity between 1860 and 1880, and their mileage now exceeds that of all of Europe combined. In 1899 the total mileage of the United States was 189,295 miles, as against 172,621 in Europe, constituting 39.4 per cent of the entire railroad system of the world. These comparative statistics are not, however, an accurate index of the relative transportation facilities, because of the greater distances which separate the important railroad centers of the United States, and the sparsity of the population in many sections, compared with the density of population in the principal countries of Europe. Notwithstanding these disadvantages, the railroad systems of the United States are so highly organized and so efficiently managed that the transportation of freight by rail is cheaper than in any other country. There have been extraordinary reductions in freight rates during the past thirty years. The average rates per ton mile on the trunk railroads of the country have declined from about 2 cents to 6 mills, and on two of them to 3.6 mills. In 1868 the freight on wheat from Chicago to New York by rail was 42.6 cents per bushel, compared with 11.55 cents per bushel in 1898. In 1877 the cost of sending 100 pounds of wheat from St. Louis to New York was 41 cents, as compared with 22.3 cents in 1898.

4. *Freedom of Interstate Commerce.*—These exceptional transportation facilities are utilized in the interchange of products between states and territories covering an area of 2,970,230 square miles of land surface, possessing a population of 75,994,575, and not separated by any commercial barrier. The mainland of the United States is the largest area in the civilized world which is thus unrestricted by customs, excises, or national prejudice, and its population possesses, because of its great collective wealth, a larger consuming capacity than that of any other nation. Statements of this character are confirmed by statistics for 1900 which show that the value of agricultural products was

$4,739,118,752, of manufactured products $13,004,400,143, and of mining products $1,067,605,587, a total of $18,811,-124,482, which was all consumed at home, except the sum of $1,370,763,571, representing the value of all articles of domestic merchandise exported in the year 1900. As a partial offset to this deduction there may be added the imports of merchandise in the same year, the value of which was $849,941,184.

5. *Freedom from Tradition.* Another advantage which has contributed to the rapid development of manufactures in the U. S. is the comparative freedom from inherited and over-conservative ideas. This country entered upon its industrial development unfettered by the old orders of things, and with a tendency on the part of the people to seek the best and quickest way to accomplish every object.

In all of the European countries in which manufacturing is an important industry, the transition from the household to the factory system was hampered by guilds, elaborate national and local restrictions, and by the natural reluctance with which a people accustomed for generations to fixed methods of work, in which they had acquired a large degree of skill, abandoned those methods for new ones. . . . This inherited and intuitive adherence to old fashioned methods is illustrated by the silk industry in France, where the handloom still predominates over the power loom; and by the tin plate industry in Wales, where until recently, hand methods of production were still in force.

In the U. S. the tendency of the artisan class to abandon the slow hand processes has been as strong as the tendency elsewhere has been to adhere to them. Moreover, there has developed among the laboring classes in the U. S. a mobility such as is unknown elsewhere in the world. . . .

29

THE GOLD STANDARD ACT OF MARCH 14, 1900 [28]

The Republican victory in the election of 1896, the return of prosperity, and the mining of new gold in the Yukon and South Africa, permitted the United States once and for all to settle the silver question. It did so in the Gold Standard Act of 1900, when silver was finally and irrevocably demonetized. Also, the Treasury's gold reserve was fixed at $150 million. By this final step, the money question once and for all was ended, the agrarian interests which had pressed for a cheap currency for more than three decades were denied relief—and an era was over.

✓   ✓   ✓

Be it enacted by the Senate and House of Representatives of the United States of America in Congress assembled, That the dollar consisting of twenty-five and three-tenths grains of gold nine-tenths fine . . . shall be the standard unit of value and all forms of money issued or coined by the United States shall be maintained at a parity of value with this standard and it shall be the duty of the Secretary of the Treasury to maintain such parity. . . .

SEC. 2. That United States notes and Treasury notes . . . when presented to the Treasury for redemption shall be redeemed in gold coin of the standard fixed and in order to secure the prompt and certain redemption of such notes as herein provided it shall be the duty of the Secretary of

[28] *U. S. Statutes at Large,* Vol. 31, 56th Congress, 1st Session, Ch. 41, p. 46.

the Treasury to set apart in the Treasury a reserve fund of one hundred and fifty million dollars in gold coin and bullion, which fund shall be used for such redemption purposes only, and whenever and as often as any of said notes shall be redeemed from said fund it shall be the duty of the Secretary of the Treasury to use said notes so redeemed to restore and maintain such reserve fund in the manner following, to wit: First, by exchanging the notes so redeemed for any gold coin in the general fund of the Treasury; second, by accepting deposits of gold coin at the Treasury or at any subtreasury in exchange for the United States notes so redeemed; third, by procuring gold coin by the use of said notes, in accordance with the provisions of section thirty-seven hundred of the Revised Statutes of the United States. If the Secretary of the Treasury is unable to restore and maintain the gold coin in the reserve fund by the foregoing methods, and the amount of such gold coin and bullion in said fund shall at any time fall below one hundred million dollars, then it shall be his duty to restore the same to the maximum sum of one hundred and fifty million dollars by borrowing money on the credit of the United States, and for the debt thus incurred to issue and sell coupon or registered bonds of the United States, in such form as he may prescribe, in denominations of fifty dollars or any multiple thereof, bearing interest at the rate of not exceeding three per centum per annum, payable quarterly, such bonds to be payable at the pleasure of the United States after one year from the date of their issue, and to be payable, principal and interest, in gold coin of the present standard value, and to be exempt from the payment of all taxes or duties of the United States, as well as from taxation in any form by or under State, municipal, or local authority; and the gold coin received from the sale of said bonds shall first be covered into the general fund of the Treasury and then exchanged, in the manner hereinbefore provided, for an equal amount of the notes redeemed and held for exchange, and the Secretary of the Treasury may, in his discretion, use said notes in exchange for gold, or to purchase or redeem any bonds of the United States, or for any other lawful purpose the public interests may require, except that they shall not be used to meet deficiencies in the current revenues. That United States notes when redeemed in accordance with the provisions of this section shall be reissued, but shall be held in the reserve fund until exchanged for gold, as herein provided; and the gold coin and bullion in the reserve fund, together with the redeemed notes held for use as provided in this section, shall at no time exceed the maximum sum of one hundred and fifty million dollars.

SEC. 3. That nothing contained in this Act shall be construed to affect the legal-tender quality as now provided by law of the silver dollar, or of any other money coined or issued by the United States. . . .

SEC. 14. That the provisions of this Act are not intended to preclude the accomplishment of international bimetallism whenever conditions shall make it expedient and practicable to secure the same by concurrent action of the leading commercial nations of the world and at a ratio which shall insure permanence of relative value between gold and silver. . . .

30

SENATOR LODGE ON IMMIGRATION RESTRICTION, MARCH 16, 1896[29]

After the Civil War, with expanding opportunities for employment in American business enterprise, hundreds of thousands of European immigrants began to pour into the United States each year. Some were the highly skilled mechanics and artisans who were notably welcomed in iron and steel, machine-tools, and the mining industries. The great majority were young men and women without training in industry but willing to work in the new factories and mills of the exploding industrial economy of the United States. Without this vast augmentation of the labor supply, the rapid strides the United States made would have been impossible. Until 1880, these immigrants had come from northern and western Europe, from nations that resembled the United States in religion and the practice of constitutional government. The decade of the eighties saw the first great waves of immigration from southern and eastern Europe. Italians, Slavs, and Russian Jews replaced English, German, and Scandinavian immigrants. Toward them hostility developed from two quarters: from organized labor, which worried about the competition of this cheaper European labor; and from sociologists who equated the crowding of slums in the cities by these newcomers with poverty, crime, and low standards of living. Senator Henry Cabot Lodge of Massachusetts (the same Lodge who was to fight President Wilson on American entry into the

[29] *Congressional Record*, 54th Congress, 1st Session. The Senate (March 16, 1896).

*League of Nations in 1919) was concerned about some-
thing else—the maintenance of the "racial" purity of
America. He introduced a bill to restrict immigration—
based on a literacy test—in the Senate; and he made the
following long speech in which he exalted the Anglo-
Saxon "race" and its mission.*

✓   ✓   ✓

MR. LODGE. Mr. President, this bill is intended to amend
the existing law so as to restrict still further immigration
to the United States. Paupers, diseased persons, convicts,
and contract laborers are now excluded. By this bill it is
proposed to make a new class of excluded immigrants and
add to those which have just been named the totally ignorant. The bill is of the simplest kind. The first section ex-
cludes from the country all immigrants who can not read
and write either their own or some other language. The
second section merely provides a simple test for determin-
ing whether the immigrant can read or write, and is added
to the bill so as to define the duties of the immigrant in-
spectors, and to assure to all immigrants alike perfect
justice and a fair test of their knowledge.

Two questions arise in connection with this bill. The
first is as to the merits of this particular form of restriction; the second as to the general policy of restricting
immigration at all. I desire to discuss briefly these two
questions in the order in which I have stated them. The
smaller question as to the merits of this particular bill
comes first. The existing laws of the United States now
exclude, as I have said, certain classes of immigrants who,
it is universally agreed, would be most undesirable additions to our population. These exclusions have been enforced and the results have been beneficial, but the excluded
classes are extremely limited and do not by any means
cover all or even any considerable part of the immigrants
whose presence here is undesirable or injurious, nor do
they have any adequate effect in properly reducing the
great body of immigration to this country. There can be
no doubt that there is a very earnest desire on the part of
the American people to restrict further and much more
extensively than has yet been done foreign immigration to
the United States. The question before the committee was

how this could best be done; that is, by what method the largest number of undesirable immigrants and the smallest possible number of desirable immigrants could be shut out. Three methods of obtaining this further restriction have been widely discussed of late years and in various forms have been brought to the attention of Congress. The first was the imposition of a capitation tax on all immigrants. There can be no doubt as to the effectiveness of this method if the tax is made sufficiently heavy. But although exclusion by a tax would be thorough, it would be undiscriminating, and your committee did not feel that the time had yet come for its application. The second scheme was to restrict immigration by requiring consular certification of immigrants. This plan has been much advocated, and if it were possible to carry it out thoroughly and to add very largely to the number of our consuls in order to do so, it would no doubt be effective and beneficial. But the committee was satisfied that consular certification was, under existing circumstances, impractical; that the necessary machinery could not be provided; that it would lead to many serious questions with foreign governments, and that it could not be properly and justly enforced. . . .

The third method was to exclude all immigrants who could neither read nor write, and this is the plan which was adopted by the committee and which is embodied in this bill. In their report the committee have shown by statistics, which have been collected and tabulated with great care, the emigrants who would be affected by this illiteracy test. It is not necessary for me here to do more than summarize the results of the committee's investigation, which have been set forth fully in their report. It is found, in the first place, that the illiteracy test will bear most heavily upon the Italians, Russians, Poles, Hungarians, Greeks, and Asiatics, and very lightly, or not at all, upon English-speaking emigrants or Germans, Scandinavians, and French. In other words, the races most affected by the illiteracy test are those whose emigration to this country has begun within the last twenty years and swelled rapidly to enormous proportions, races with which the English-speaking people have never hitherto assimilated, and who are most alien to the great body of the people of the United States. On the other hand, immigrants from the United Kingdom and of those races which are most closely related to the English-speaking people, and who with the English-speaking people themselves founded the American colonies and built up the United States, are affected but little by the proposed test. These races would not be prevented by this law from coming to this country in practically undiminished numbers. These kindred races also are those who alone go to the Western and Southern States, where immigrants are desired, and take up our unoccupied lands. The races which would suffer most seriously by exclusion under the proposed bill furnish the immigrants who do not go to the West or South, where immigration is needed, but who remain on the Atlantic Seaboard, where immigration is not needed and where their presence is most injurious and undesirable.

The statistics prepared by the committee show further that the immigrants excluded by the illiteracy test are those who remain for the most part in congested masses in our great cities. They furnish, as other tables show, a large proportion of the population of the slums. The committee's report proves that illiteracy runs parallel with the slum population, with criminals, paupers, and juvenile delinquents of foreign birth or parentage, whose percentage is out of all proportion to their share of the total population when compared with the percentage of the same classes among the native born. It also appears from investigations which have been made that the immigrants who would be shut out by the illiteracy test are those who bring least money to the country and come most quickly upon private or public charity for support. . . .

These facts prove to demonstration that the exclusion of immigrants unable to read or write, as proposed by this bill, will operate against the most undesirable and harmful part of our present immigration and shut out elements which no thoughtful or patriotic man can wish to see multiplied among the people of the United States. The report of the committee also proves that this bill meets the great requirement of all legislation of this character in excluding the greatest proportion possible of thoroughly undesirable and dangerous immigrants and the smallest proportion of immigrants who are unobjectionable.

I have said enough to show what the effects of this bill

would be, and that if enacted into law it would be fair in its operation and highly beneficial in its results. It now remains for me to discuss the second and larger question, as to the advisability of restricting immigration at all. This is a subject of the greatest magnitude and the most far-reaching importance. It has two sides, the economic and the social. As to the former, but few words are necessary. There is no one thing which does so much to bring about a reduction of wages and to injure the American wage earner as the unlimited introduction of cheap foreign labor through unrestricted immigration. Statistics show that the change in the race character of our immigration has been accompanied by a corresponding decline in its quality. The number of skilled mechanics and of persons trained to some occupation or pursuit has fallen off, while the number of those without occupation or training, that is, who are totally unskilled, has risen in our recent immigration to enormous proportions. This low, unskilled labor is the most deadly enemy of the American wage earner, and does more than anything else toward lowering his wages and forcing down his standard of living. An attempt was made, with the general assent of both political parties, to meet this crying evil some years ago by the passage of what are known as the contract-labor laws. That legislation was excellent in intention, but has proved of but little value in practice. It has checked to a certain extent the introduction of cheap, low-class labor in large masses into the United States. It has made it a little more difficult for such labor to come here, but the labor of this class continues to come, even if not in the same way, and the total amount of it has not been materially reduced. Even if the contract-labor laws were enforced intelligently and thoroughly, there is no reason to suppose that they would have any adequate effect in checking the evil which they were designed to stop. It is perfectly clear after the experience of several years that the only relief which can come to the American wage earner from the competition of low-class immigrant labor must be by general laws restricting the total amount of immigration and framed in such a way as to affect most strongly those elements of the immigration which furnish the low, unskilled, and ignorant foreign labor. . . .

I now come to the aspect of this question which is graver and more serious than any other. The injury of unrestricted immigration to American wages and American standards of living is sufficiently plain and is bad enough, but the danger which this immigration threatens to the quality of our citizenship is far worse. That which it concerns us to know and that which is more vital to us as a people than all possible questions of tariff or currency is whether the quality of our citizenship is endangered by the present course and character of immigration to the United States. To determine this question intelligently we must look into the history of our race. . . .

For practical purposes in considering a question of race and in dealing with the civilized peoples of western Europe and of America there is no such thing as a race of original purity according to the divisions of ethnical science. In considering the practical problems of the present time we can deal only with artificial races—that is, races like the English-speaking people, the French, or the Germans— who have been developed as races by the operation during a long period of time of climactic influences, wars, migrations, conquests, and industrial development. To the philologist and the ethnologist it is of great importance to determine the ethnical divisions of mankind in the earliest historic times. To the scientific modern historian, to the student of social phenomena, and to the statesman alike the early ethnic divisions are of little consequence, but the sharply marked race divisions which have been gradually developed by the conditions and events of the last thousand years are absolutely vital. It is by these conditions and events that the races or nations which to-day govern the world have been produced, and it is their characteristics which it is important for us to understand.

How, then, has the English-speaking race, which to-day controls so large a part of the earth's surface, been formed? Great Britain and Ireland at the time of the Roman conquest were populated by Celtic tribes. After the downfall of the Roman Empire these tribes remained in possession of the islands with probably but a very slight infusion of Latin blood. Then came what is commonly known as the Saxon invasion. Certain North German tribes, own brothers to those other tribes which

swept southward and westward over the whole Roman
Empire, crossed the English Channel and landed in the
corner of England known as the Isle of Thanet. They were
hard fighters, pagans, and adventurers. They swept over
the whole of England and the Lowlands of Scotland. A
few British words like basket, relating to domestic employments, indicate that only women of the conquered race,
and not many of those, were spared. The extermination
was fierce and thorough. The native Celts were driven
back into the Highlands of Scotland and to the edge of
the sea in Cornwall and Wales, while all the rest of the
land became Saxon.

The conquerors established themselves in their new
country, were converted to Christianity, and began to
advance in civilization. Then came a fresh wave from the
Germanic tribes. This time it was the Danes. They were
of the same blood as the Saxons, and the two kindred
races fought hard for the possession of England until the
last comers prevailed and their chiefs reached the throne.
Then in 1066 there was another invasion, this time from
the shores of France. But the new invaders and conquerors
were not Frenchmen. As Carlyle says, they were only
Saxons who spoke French. A hundred years before these
Normans, or Northmen, northernmost of all the Germanic tribes, had descended from their land of snow
and ice upon Europe. They were the most remarkable
of all the people who poured out of the Germanic forests. They came upon Europe in their long, low ships,
a set of fighting pirates and buccaneers, and yet these
same pirates brought with them out of the darkness and
cold of the north a remarkable literature and a strange
and poetic mythology. Wherever they went they conquered, and wherever they stopped they set up for themselves dukedoms, principalities, and kingdoms. To them
we owe the marvels of Gothic architecture, for it was they
who were the great builders and architects of mediæval
Europe. They were great military engineers as well and
revived the art of fortified defense, which had been lost to
the world. They were great statesmen and great generals,
and they had only been in Normandy about a hundred
years when they crossed the English Channel, conquered
the country, and gave to England for many generations to

come her kings and nobles. But the Normans in their turn were absorbed or blended with the great mass of the Danes and the still earlier Saxons. . . .

When the Reformation came this work was pretty nearly done, and after that great movement had struck off the shackles from the human mind the English-speaking people were ready to come forward and begin to play their part in a world where the despotism of the church had been broken, and where political despotism was about to enter on its great struggle against the forces of freedom. . . .

This period, when the work of centuries which had resulted in the making of the English people was complete, and when they were entering upon their career of world conquest, is of peculiar interest to us. Then it was that from the England of Shakespeare and Bacon and Raleigh, and later from the England of Pym and Hampden and Cromwell and Milton, Englishmen fared forth across the great ocean to the North American Continent. The first Englishmen to come here settled on the James River, and there laid the foundation of the great State of Virginia. The next landed much farther to the north. . . .

Such, then, briefly, were the people composing the colonies when we faced England in the war for independence. It will be observed that with the exception of the Huguenot French, who formed but a small percentage of the total population, the people of the thirteen colonies were all of the same original race stocks. The Dutch, the Swedes, and the Germans simply blended again with the English-speaking people, who like them were descended from the Germanic tribes whom Cæsar fought and Tacitus described.

During the present century, down to 1875, there have been three large migrations to this country in addition to the always steady stream from Great Britain; one came from Ireland about the middle of the century, and somewhat later one from Germany and one from Scandinavia, in which is included Sweden, Denmark, and Norway. The Irish, although of a different race stock originally, have been closely associated with the English-speaking people for nearly a thousand years. They speak the same language, and during that long period the two races have lived side by side, and to some extent intermarried. The

Germans and Scandinavians are again people of the same race stock as the English who founded and built up the colonies. During this century, down to 1875, then, as in the two which preceded it, there had been scarcely any immigration to this country, except from kindred or allied races, and no other, which was sufficiently numerous to have produced any effect on the national characteristics, or to be taken into account here. Since 1875, however, there has been a great change. While the people who for two hundred and fifty years have been migrating to America have continued to furnish large numbers of immigrants to the United States, other races of totally different race origin, with whom the English-speaking people have never hitherto been assimilated or brought in contact, have suddenly begun to immigrate to the United States in large numbers. Russians, Hungarians, Poles, Bohemians, Italians, Greeks, and even Asiatics, whose immigration to America was almost unknown twenty years ago, have during the last twenty years poured in in steadily increasing numbers, until now they nearly equal the immigration of those races kindred in blood or speech, or both, by whom the United States has hitherto been built up and the American people formed.

This momentous fact is the one which confronts us today, and if continued, it carries with it future consequences far deeper than any other event of our times. It involves, in a word, nothing less than the possibility of a great and perilous change in the very fabric of our race. The English-speaking race, as I have shown, has been made slowly during the centuries. Nothing has happened thus far to radically change it here. In the United States, after allowing for the variations produced by new climatic influences and changed conditions of life and of political institutions, it is still in the great essentials fundamentally the same race. The additions in this country until the present time have been from kindred people or from those with whom we have been long allied and who speak the same language. By those who look at this question superficially we hear it often said that the English-speaking people, especially in America, are a mixture of races. Analysis shows that the actual mixture of blood in the English-speaking race is very small, and that while the English-speaking people are derived through different channels, no doubt, there is among them none the less an overwhelming preponderance of the same race stock, that of the great Germanic tribes who reached from Norway to the Alps. They have been welded together by more than a thousand years of wars, conquests, migrations, and struggles, both at home and abroad, and in so doing they have attained a fixity and definiteness of national character unknown to any other people. . . .

It being admitted, therefore, that a historic race of fixed type has been developed, it remains to consider what this means, what a race is, and what a change would portend. That which identifies a race and sets it apart from others is not to be found merely or ultimately in its physical appearance, its institutions, its laws, its literature, or even its language. These are in the last analysis only the expression or the evidence of race. The achievements of the intellect pass easily from land to land and from people to people. The telephone, invented but yesterday, is used to-day in China, in Australia, or in South Africa as freely as in the United States. The book which the press to-day gives to the world in English is scattered to-morrow throughout the earth in every tongue, and the thoughts of the writer become the property of mankind. You can take a Hindoo and give him the highest education the world can afford. He has a keen intelligence. He will absorb the learning of Oxford, he will acquire the manners and habits of England, he will sit in the British Parliament, but you can not make him an Englishman. Yet he, like his conqueror, is of the great Indo-European family. But it has taken six thousand years and more to create the differences which exist between them. You can not efface those differences thus made, by education in a single life, because they do not rest upon the intellect. What, then, is this matter of race which separates the Englishman from the Hindoo and the American from the Indian? It is something deeper and more fundamental than anything which concerns the intellect. We all know it instinctively, although it is so impalpable that we can scarcely define it, and yet is so deeply marked that even the physiological differences between the Negro, the Mongol, and the Caucasian are not more persistent or more obvious.

When we speak of a race, then, we do not mean its expressions in art or in language, or its achievements in knowledge. We mean the moral and intellectual characters, which in their association make the soul of a race, and which represent the product of all its past, the inheritance of all its ancestors, and the motives of all its conduct. The men of each race possess an indestructible stock of ideas, traditions, sentiments, modes of thought, an unconscious inheritance from their ancestors, upon which argument has no effect. What makes a race are their mental and, above all, their moral characteristics, the slow growth and accumulation of centuries of toil and conflict. These are the qualities which determine their social efficiency as a people, which make one race rise and another fall, which we draw out of a dim past through many generations of ancestors, about which we can not argue, but in which we blindly believe, and which guide us in our short-lived generation as they have guided the race itself across the centuries. . . .

Such achievements as M. Le Bon credits us with are due to the qualities of the American people, whom he, as a man of science looking below the surface, rightly describes as homogeneous. Those qualities are moral far more than intellectual, and it is on the moral qualities of the English-speaking race that our history, our victories, and all our future rest. There is only one way in which you can lower those qualities or weaken those characteristics, and that is by breeding them out. If a lower race mixes with a higher in sufficient numbers, history teaches us that the lower race will prevail. The lower race will absorb the higher, not the higher the lower, when the two strains approach equality in numbers. In other words, there is a limit to the capacity of any race for assimilating and elevating an inferior race, and when you begin to pour in in unlimited numbers people of alien or lower races of less social efficiency and less moral force, you are running the most frightful risk that any people can run. The lowering of a great race means not only its own decline but that of human civilization. M. Le Bon sees no danger to us in immigration, and his reason for this view is one of the most interesting things he says. He declares that the people of the United States will never be injured by immigration, because the moment they see the peril the great race instinct will assert itself and shut the immigration out. The reports of the Treasury for the last fifteen years show that the peril is at hand. I trust that the prediction of science is true and that the unerring instinct of the race will shut the danger out, as it closed the door upon the coming of the Chinese. . . .

Mr. President, more precious even than forms of government are the mental and moral qualities which make what we call our race. While those stand unimpaired all is safe. When those decline all is imperiled. They are exposed to but a single danger, and that is by changing the quality of our race and citizenship through the wholesale infusion of races whose traditions and inheritances, whose thoughts and whose beliefs are wholly alien to ours and with whom we have never assimilated or even been associated in the past. The danger has begun. It is small as yet, comparatively speaking, but it is large enough to warn us to act while there is yet time and while it can be done easily and efficiently. There lies the peril at the portals of our land; there is pressing in the tide of unrestricted immigration. The time has certainly come, if not to stop, at least to check, to sift, and to restrict those immigrants. In careless strength, with generous hand, we have kept our gates wide open to all the world. If we do not close them, we should at least place sentinels beside them to challenge those who would pass through. The gates which admit men to the United States and to citizenship in the great Republic should no longer be left unguarded.

31

INDUSTRIAL AMERICA, 1884-85 [30]

In the 1880's, as a result of the demands of the Knights of Labor (it was their only substantial victory despite their existence for more than 20 years), Congress created the Bureau of Labor in the Department of Interior to gather facts about wages and working conditions. President Arthur named Carroll D. Wright—one of the country's early students of labor problems—America's first Labor Commissioner and instructed him to inquire into the cause and nature of industrial depressions. (The United States had gone through a prolonged one during 1873-79, and a briefer one during 1884-85.) For his first report, Wright collected a vast array of statistical data; his materials were filled with lacunae and his techniques of analysis—by present-day standards—were quite primitive. But his data do show the relations between unemployment and the extraordinary technological fluidity of a rapidly growing industrial economy. So impressed was Wright by these achievements that he ventured a prediction: the Western World, in terms of technological progress, was nearing maturity; there seemed few worlds left to conquer. Here Wright seemed to be anticipating the "maturity school" of American economists (that is, those who were following J. M. Keynes) of 50 years later.

1   1   1

[30] *First Annual Report of the Commissioner of Labor, Industrial Depressions* (Washington, 1886).

CHAPTER III: THE MANUFACTURING NATIONS CONSIDERED AS A GROUP IN RELATION TO THE PRESENT DEPRESSION

IT IS APPARENT from the statistical illustrations given in the preceding chapters that the family of manufacturing states, Great Britain, France, Belgium, Germany, and the United States, if not also Austria, Russia, and Italy, are suffering from an industrial depression novel in its kind, and yet having characteristic features of similarity throughout the whole range of states. It seems to be quite true that in those states considered the volume of business and of production has not been affected disastrously by the depression, but that prices have been greatly reduced, wages frequently reduced, and margins of profits carried to the minimum range. Over-production seems to prevail in all alike without regard to the system of commerce which exists in either. What has brought all these states to the position in which they are found at the present time constitutes a most interesting and important question in economics, and one vitally affecting the wage-workers of the world. The wide study given to this matter has resulted in some conclusions entirely warranted by the facts, which may not be lacking in value, and not only the facts, but the results of the facts, are properly stated at this point.

If each of these great communities has reached an industrial condition involving phases common to all, there must be somewhere a line of reasons for such universal condition, and one should be able to develop the logical course of events which has brought such a wide range of states to an industrial epoch.

England, with generations of skill in mechanical employment, was the first to establish the factory system and institute a new industrial order of things, in which the division of labor became more and more an important factor. She controlled also the exchange of the world. In her insular position she was able to make the world pay tribute to her by compelling the produce of the world to pass through her hands, either in kind or in settlement of balances. With these immense advantages, and having the control, too, of raw materials in abundance, it was natural

that England should seek to supply the world with manufactured products. This she was able to do with the aid of
her skill, of her science, of rapid transportation, which she
did much to develop, and of the vast capital which she possessed, enabling her to carry on great enterprises. So her
ambition was natural and legitimate, and her great prosperity came to her without regard to any commercial system which she might have established, and in spite of
commercial systems. Free trade became to her a necessity,
because she sold to the world her manufactured products,
and the world had few manufactured products to sell to
her. With the constant increase of equipment to carry out
her industrial policy, England at last found herself, on
account of the course of other nations, with a plant altogether too large for the demands made upon her, and with
a capacity sufficient to supply not only all her own home
and colonial markets but a great share of the other markets
of the world.

The United States, after the war of the Revolution,
found that political freedom only had been secured as the
result of the war. Industrially this country was under the
control of Great Britain. It became essential to establish
a commercial system, which it was thought would enable
our industries to become gradually free from the industrial control of England. This policy has, with few interruptions, been pursued to the present time. Foreign
producers of manufactured goods have gradually lost the
American market, and the American producers have
gradually found themselves in position to supply the home
demand. Stimulated in this direction, the United States
has gone on perfecting machinery, duplicating plant,
crowding the market with products, until to-day this country is in the exact position of England, with productive
capacity far in excess of the demand upon it, and her industries, as those of Great Britain, stagnated, the wages
of labor reduced, prices lowered, and the manufacturers
and merchants trying to secure an outlet for surplus goods.
This condition has been reached under a system the reverse
of that which has prevailed in England, and while stimulation has been enhanced by the system prevailing here,
the condition has been reached in spite of it.

France, at first drawing her skilled workmen from England and tardy in the establishment of the factory system, at last concluded she ought to supply her own markets at least, and so began war on British industry. With a natural ambition to supply her own markets, she has carried the stimulation so far that she has not only secured the capacity to supply herself but has a vastly enhanced capacity, and is seeking to supply others. To-day France finds herself, through her policy, in precisely the same industrial situation that attends Great Britain and America.

Germany has followed the example of France and the United States, and with precisely the same results. Her commercial policy or system has been, of late years, the same as that of the United States, while Belgium has followed that of Great Britain, and yet all these nations now find themselves in sympathy in their distress, all seeking outlets for their surplus production. The scale of wages in the countries named is according to the following order, the highest first: The United States, Great Britain, France, Belgium, Germany. It is difficult to connect commercial systems with this scale of wages, and when the broad view is taken that each of these countries has overstocked itself with machinery and manufacturing plant far in excess of the wants of production, and when it is considered also that the present period of industrial depression is unique in its character, as not having been attended with financial and commercial crises and panics, financial matters having been only incidentally involved, and when it is considered further that the condition of these nations has been reached under both free trade and protective policies, and under a wide range of tariff restrictions, it is readily seen that the family of nations given to mechanical production have reached an epoch in their existence, and that commercial systems which might have been at one time, or under some circumstances, necessities, are now apparently only expediencies, to be used temporarily and not as permanent features of national progress. Historically, it must be admitted that the two great opposing systems of free trade and protection have played well their parts in the industrial development of nations; but the wisdom derived from the experience of all the nations in the race for industrial success should teach each that ultimately that system freest from restrictions will beget generally the best conditions. Meantime, expediency has its power, and must continue to exercise it until the evil resulting from changes can be met through the softening influences which come from contest and hardship. The struggle so far has had a strong influence in producing ever recurring periods of depression. These considerations are shown to be valid through the information collected by the Bureau in all the countries involved. . . .

In England, Belgium, and France the railroads and canals that are really needed have been built. There remains only to be constructed feeding and competing lines, and experience shows that for such lines the revenue for the capital invested is not equal to nominal remuneration. In Holland the great works are completed; Amsterdam is united to the sea, international communications have been well established, and there are no longer urgent works to be undertaken, and the reward of capital to be invested now is not sufficient to tempt lenders. In Italy and Spain the great arteries are provided with railroads, while the products moved and the revenues derived from capital invested are notoriously inferior to what was expected. When this is the case there is no prospect of rival or subsidiary lines being constructed. Harbors and rivers are sufficiently developed, and warehouses, water and gas works, tramways, etc., are largely provided for. The Pyrenees and the Alps are tunnelled, and a sufficient network of international communication established. In England railroad building cannot be extended to a sufficient degree to absorb much capital or much labor. In Russia the principal lines of railroad have been built with the aid of the Government, and it is not likely that further construction will take place except for strategical purposes. Germany is provided with a full network of railroads, and the facilities for transportation are in excess of actual needs. Austria is in much the same condition as Germany, and Turkey also has as many railroads as can be used. In the United States the mileage of new railroads constructed has been out of all proportion to the increase of the products to be carried.

The Suez Canal has been built, terrestrial and transoceanic lines of telegraph have been laid, and the merchant marine has been transformed from wood to iron. To-day the carrying service of nations, and especially of the great marine nation, England, is overstocked to a far greater extent than the industries. On all sides one sees the accomplished result of the labor of half a century. From a financial point of view, these accomplished results should always be good, but in many cases it is apparent that undertakings have proved deceptive and Governments become needy and some, as Egypt, insolvent. Whatever may have been the financial results, industry has been enormously developed, cities have been transformed, distances covered, and a new set of economic tools has been given in profusion to rich countries, and in a more reasonable amount to poorer ones. What is strictly necessary has been done oftentimes to superfluity. This full supply of economic tools to meet the wants of nearly all branches of commerce and industry is the most important factor in the present industrial depression. It is true that the discovery of new processes of manufacture will undoubtedly continue, and this will act as an ameliorating influence, but it will not leave room for a marked extension, such as has been witnessed during the last fifty years, or afford a remunerative employment of the vast amount of capital which has been created during that period. The market price of products will continue low, no matter what the cost of production may be. The day of large profits is probably past. There may be room for further intensive, but not extensive, development of industry in the present area of civilization. Outside of the area of a high state of industrial civilization, in China, Japan, India, Australia, Persia, and South Africa, there is a vast deal to be done, but this of necessity will be accomplished slowly, as these countries, not having the capital to make speculative movements, must depend upon the money-lending countries. Supplying themselves with full facilities for industries and commerce will give to each of the great nations of Europe and of America something to do, but the part of each in this work will be small and far from enough to insure more than temporary activity. It may help to keep away stagnation and modify the severity and the duration of industrial depressions. There are very many influences, like the great expense of standing armies, of war and revolutions, and local features, so far as causes are concerned, which enter into the consideration of the industrial situation of the world so far as localities are specifically concerned. The present treatment only has to do with those things which seem to be common. The building of railroads and of ships, even in countries where the land is interlaced with roads and supplied with wharfs lined with shipping, must go on, because the waste needs repairing, and the great industrial work of supplying the world will furnish enough for all to do; but the brief review of the present industrial situation of the great communities involved indicates that statesmanship is required to establish such guards and checks in human affairs as shall lead to a safer and surer progress than that which has attended the past decade. In the consideration of suggested remedies and in the summary of this report facts will be brought out which will at least be suggestive of channels into which legislation, but more effectually public sentiment, may be directed. Certainly, with the aid of the wisdom of some of the best minds in Europe and America, and of men having the largest experience, these directions should have their influence.

One of the agents of the Bureau reports as the result of interviews had with leading economists in Europe the following as the predominant features of modern industrial development among the producing nations: (1) The influence of the increased facilities for transportation and international communication. (2) The steady progress of rising wages, contemporaneous with declining profits. (3) The enlargement of the circle of producing nations to such extent as to make the means of production far in excess of the needs of consumption. The factors responsible for this state of affairs are—

(a) The desire to participate in the large profits made by those first in the field.

(b) The continuous flow of precious metals after the discovery of the gold mines of California and Australia.

(c) The extension of the credit system, facilitating the advance of capital to those who knew the processes and secrets of manufacture, but who had not the ready money to commence business on their own account.

(d) The establishment of protective tariffs in most of

the western European countries and the United States in-
ducing sharp domestic competition and over-production.

(e) The abnormal stimulus given to industry in Germany by the accomplishment of German unity and by the
payment by the Government of its domestic obligations
from the war indemnity received from France. . . .

— 32 —

LABOR, WAGES, AND TECHNOLOGY, 1895 [31]

Wright, who had been so uncertain about America's continued economic advance in the 1880's, ten years later was to change his mind. Thanks to machine production, worker productivity was increasing enormously and so were the wealth and income of the United States. But labor was also profiting: in more wages, in a shorter working day and—best of all—in higher real wages as a result of lower costs for necessities due to machine production. This was one of the early awarenesses by a contemporary of a key factor in America's great industrial progress after the Civil War—technology—and its consequences to the whole economy. Rather than being exploited (despite the dire predictions of Karl Marx), American labor apparently was receiving its fair share of the national income. Wright was able to use the statistics on wages and prices collected by the Senate Committee on Finance and published in its report on "Wholesale Prices and Wages" (Senate Report No. 1394, 52nd Congress, 2nd Session).

✓   ✓   ✓

CHAPTER XVII: LABOR AND RATES OF WAGES, 1790-1890

A statement of the actual or average wages for any period or locality, especially when used for purposes of comparison, is not complete unless accompanied by information as to the hours of labor, regulations as to extra

[31] Wright, Carroll D., *Industrial Evolution of the United States* (New York, 1895).

earnings, division of earnings among underhands, and other methods peculiar to the period or locality. Information as to cost of living and prices of commodities should also be considered, since it is not the amount of money wages that most nearly concerns the workman, but the amount of subsistence obtainable at a given period for a given expenditure. This chapter, however, is confined chiefly to a presentation of wages, prices being incidentally treated. The rates selected are either actual wages or the average for a number of establishments in different localities, and it is believed they fairly represent the wages for the different classes of labor. While the rate of wages for the same class of employees in different establishments within a given district may vary, the tendency is to equality.

In giving wages and prices for the past one hundred years, especially for the first half of the century, recourse has been chiefly to Eastern and Middle State conditions. This has been necessitated by the lack of data for other portions of the country, but it is believed that the facts given are fairly representative relatively of variations in all manufacturing districts of the country taken as a whole, notwithstanding the great variations occurring between one part of the country and another.

At the beginning of the constitutional period, as stated in the chapter on wages in colonial days, not much change had been experienced in the rates of wages paid in different trades, but between 1790 and 1830, when the factory system was in fair and general operation and labor of every character commanded higher wages, it being in greater demand, there was a fair advance, carpenters in 1790 being paid less than 60 cents a day; in 1800 something over 70 cents; in 1810, $1.09 on the average; in 1820, $1.13; in 1830, about $1.13, reaching, however, in the northern parts of our country an average of $1.40 a day during the period from 1830 to 1840. After this there was not much change for carpenters until 1860. Taking laborers, on the other hand, as fairly representative of general conditions, it is found that they were paid, in 1790, about 43 cents a day, on the average; in 1800, 62½ cents a day; from 1800 to 1810, about 82 cents a day; from 1810 to 1820, something over 90 cents a day, while

from 1840 to 1860 they varied from 87½ cents to $1 a
day. Printers were receiving, at the beginning of the century, about $1.00 a day, and their wages had increased to
$1.75 by 1860. Shoemakers were paid 73⅓ cents a day,
on the average, during the decennial period 1790 to 1800,
while they averaged from 1820 to 1830, $1.06 a day, reach-
ing $1.70 in 1860. Looking to cotton-mill operatives, whose
wages are not quoted much prior to 1820, we find that
they were paid 44 cents a day, on the average, between
1820 and 1830, nearly 90 cents a day from 1830 to 1840.
This wage held, with slight increase, to 1850, while during
the next decade of years their average pay was $1.03 a day.
Woolen-mill operatives did somewhat better, being paid
in the earlier part of the factory period, that is, the decade
of years prior to 1830, $1.12; they rarely reached this high
wage again before 1880.

The record of wages after 1830 is far more complete,
and the course of their rise or fall can be more clearly
stated. In 1831 daily wages for agricultural laborers
ranged from 57.5 cents to $1.00; blacksmiths received from
$1.00 to $1.25 per day. The daily average for carpenters
was $1.07, but ranged as high as $1.50, while masons received $1.26. Since 1873 wages in these staple occupations
had more than doubled, but the segregation of mechanics
and labor of all kinds into classes had made rapid progress,
and an average wage for such a broad grouping conveys
no idea of the rates of wages for the different classes. The
average daily wages for paper-mill operatives in 1831 was
66.6 cents, printers $1.25, shoemakers, $1.06, cotton-mill
operatives 88.6 cents, woolen-mill operatives 94.6 cents,
glassmakers $1.13, and millwrights $1.21.

During the thirty years from 1830 to 1860 two violent
commercial convulsions occurred, one in 1837 and one in
1857. Excessive importations, speculation, and the abuse
of the credit system were the principal causes of both these
business depressions; both had the effect of temporarily
reducing wages in certain industries. Wages had not fully
recovered from the panic of 1857 by 1860. The averages
for the decade ending that year, however, show a decided
advance over 1830. An average for the ten years ending
with 1860 gives agricultural laborers $1.01 per day, black-
smiths $1.69, carpenters $2.03, and masons $1.53; paper-

mill operatives received $1.17, printers $1.75, shoemakers $1.70, cotton-mill operatives $1.03, woolen-mill operatives 87.3 cents, glassmakers $2.96, and millwrights $1.66. The wages in all of these occupations, with the exception of woolen-mill operatives, show an advance over 1830. The percentage of increase ranges from 16.3 for cotton-mill operatives to 161.9 for glassmakers. On making a similar comparison of wages for twenty different occupations, it is found that but one shows an increase in average daily wages.

Without considering the effect that the war, the fluctuation in currency, or the financial crisis of 1873 may have had on wages during the twenty years from 1860 to 1880, we will compare the averages for 1860 with similar averages for 1880. Agricultural laborers in 1880 received $1.31 per day, blacksmiths $2.28, carpenters $2.42, masons $2.79, paper-mill operatives $2.79, printers $2.18, shoemakers $1.76, cotton-mill operatives $1.40, woolen-mill operatives $1.24, and glassmakers $1.79. These average wages for leading industries indicate the general increase in wages in all occupations during the fifty years from 1830 to 1880. . . .

Carrying this comparison of actual wages for distinct classes into the building trades, a representative establishment in New York reports the pay for carpenters in 1843 as $1.50 per day, and in 1891 $3.50, with the hours of work reduced from ten to eight. The pay of bricklayers and their helpers increased from $1.75 and $1.00, respectively, in 1851 to $4.00 and $2.50, respectively, in 1891, with a decrease of two hours in working time. The daily wages of draughtsmen and foremen blacksmiths, two widely separated yet dependent classes of labor, as reported by an establishment engaged in manufacturing metals and metallic goods in New York, increased from $1.75 and $2.50, respectively, in 1848 to $5.31 and $5.83 in 1891. Making a similar comparison for an entirely different class of wage-earners, that of railroad employees, we find the pay of locomotive engineers and firemen increasing from $2.14 and $1.06 in 1840 to $3.77 and $1.96, respectively, in 1891; during the same period the pay of passenger car conductors increased from $2.11 to $3.84. . . .

Considering the wages for the great mass of wage earners, the common and agricultural laborers, during the entire period since 1633, the daily wages for the best laborers advanced from 25 cents to 33.3 cents immediately before the Revolution, to 42.5 cents immediately after, and during June of 1891 the wages of common laborers ranged from $2.50 in Montana to 75 cents in the Carolinas and $1.25 in New York. Farm laborers received, during June, 1891, from $30 to $40 per month, with board and lodging, in Montana and California, to $9 and $10 in the Carolinas and Virginia, and $15 to $20 in New York. Masons (master workmen) received 33.3 cents per day in 1633 and $1.00 in 1790, while during the busy season of 1891 their wages ranged from $4.50 to $5.00 in California and Colorado, $2.50 in North Carolina, and $2.50 and $3.36 in Pennsylvania and New York.

The wages paid in numerous occupations can be compared, and in each instance the same, or a similar, advance is shown. The three classes given, however, are sufficient . . . to convey an idea of the great increase in the money wages of all classes of workmen during the two hundred and fifty-eight years. While the number actually employed increases or diminishes with business prosperity or depression, their employment or idleness appears to have had but little effect on the rate of pay. Wages during almost the entire period have had an upward tendency, decreases being the exception and generally only of temporary duration.

Turning from the specific wages paid in some of the leading occupations, it is interesting to study the relative percentage of increase of wages in general. This can be done by assuming that at a certain period wages can be represented by 100, or par, and then calculating the increase or decrease from par in accordance with the facts. Whatever wages were in 1860, they are quoted at 100. Starting from this basic point, it has been found that, taking the wages (which were taken from actual payrolls) in twenty-two industries and from nearly one hundred distinct establishments, and making a simple average, the percentages stood at 87.7 in 1840, as compared with 100 in 1860; that in 1866 they stood at 152.4, and in 1891 at 160.7. But it might be objected that a simple average does not indicate the general percentage of increase or decrease; so the figures have been averaged according to their importance, each industry relative to all industries, as represented by the number employed in each. On this basis, taking 1860 as represented by 100 again, it is found that the general average of wages in 1840 is represented by 82.5, in 1866 by 155.6, and in 1891 by 168.6; that is to say, on this basis wages have increased since 1860, as is shown by percentages, to the extent of 68.6 per cent; and this figure shows the course of wages in this country since that year. On the basis of 100 in 1860, the increase has been from 82.5 in 1840 to 168.6 in 1891, the close of the period discussed.

It is difficult always to make a statement concerning the course of prices for any considerable period of time that will be satisfactory to all students. The actual price of different articles does not alone indicate such course, because one article enters into the consumption of the people in slight degree, the price of such article having a wide range, while another article, entering largely into consumption, may be represented by a price quite steady; so there is always contention as to whether the price represented by the basis of consumption or the degree of consumption of each group of articles has risen or fallen.

In the Sixteenth Annual Report of the Massachusetts Bureau of Statistics of Labor there are very extensive quotations of the prices of commodities covering the period from 1752 to 1883 and general comparisons from 1830 to 1860. Without going into the details of these comparisons, it appears that from 1830 to 1860 agricultural products advanced in price 62.8 per cent; burning oils and fluids, 29 per cent; candles and soap, 42.6 per cent; dairy products, 38.8 per cent; fish, 9.8 per cent; flour and meal, 26 per cent; fuel, meaning by this wood only, 55.4 per cent; meats, which included turkey in this particular comparison, 53 per cent. On the other hand, prices declined for boots and shoes 38.9 per cent; clothing and dress goods, 24.7 per cent; dry goods, 30.9 per cent; food preparations, 17.5 per cent; letter paper, 35.1 per cent; spices and condiments, 36.5 per cent.

By a consolidation of the percentages showing either an advance or decline in prices for the fourteen classes of articles just cited, the general percentage of increase in price is found to be 9.6 per cent. If, on the other hand, the averages for the same classes of articles be considered, and not the percentages obtained for each class, it is found that the general average increase in price was 15.7 per cent. The mean of these two percentages is 12.7, and this more probably indicates the correct position of the fourteen classes of articles just named in their general tendency between 1830 and 1860.

If, however, wages for the same period, as given for the various occupations named in the report cited above, be consolidated and averaged, the general average increase shown for the period ending with 1860, as compared with that ending with 1830, is 52.3 per cent. These facts clearly indicate that for that thirty years wages advanced to a much greater degree than prices.

It is fortunate that the public can now have recourse to the report of the Senate Committee on Finance, which has been referred to. Wholesale prices are given in this report for 223 leading articles of consumption from 1840 to 1890, and taking the prices of these articles as a whole, and considering them on the same basis as that on which wages were considered, that is, assuming the quotations for 1860 to be 100, or par, it is found that the percentages are, for 1840, 97.7 per cent relatively to 100 in 1860, 187.7 for 1866, and 94.4 for 1891; or, in other words, prices generally, so far as the 223 leading articles are concerned, fell from 100 in 1860 to 94.4 in 1891.

Placing wages and prices in juxtaposition in a general comparison, it is found that wages, considered relatively to the importance of one industry to all industries, stood at 168.6 in 1891 relatively to 100 in 1860, and that the prices of 223 commodities entering into consumption, on the basis of the importance of each article in proportion to the importance of all, fell from 100 in 1860 to 94.4 in 1891. The conclusion, therefore, must be positive and absolute that, while the percentage of increase in prices rose in 1866 to a point far beyond the increase in wages, prices had, by 1891, fallen to a point lower, on the whole than they were in 1840, and wages had risen even above the high point they reached in 1866.

It should be stated that in these percentages the prices of rents have not been considered. Rents have increased greatly, but taking the rise in rents into consideration, as well as the rise in food products and some other things, and drawing a general conclusion relative to real wages, the statements just made must hold as practically and generally established. . . .

CHAPTER XXVII: THE INFLUENCE OF MACHINERY ON LABOR

In the manufacture of agricultural implements new machinery has, in the opinion of some of the best manufacturers of such implements, displaced fully fifty per cent of the muscular labor formerly employed, as, for instance, hammers and dies have done away with the most particular labor on a plow. In one of the most extensive establishments engaged in the manufacture of agricultural implements in one of the Western States it is found that 600 men, with the use of machinery, are now doing the work that would require 2,145 men, without the aid of machinery, to perform; that is to say, there has been in this particular establishment a loss of labor to 1,545 men, the proportion of loss being as 3.57 to 1.

In the manufacture of small arms, where one man, by manual labor, was formerly able to "turn" and "fit" one stock for a musket in one day of ten hours, three men now, by a division of labor and the use of power machinery, will turn out and fit from 125 to 150 stocks in ten hours. By this statement it is seen that one man individually turns out and fits the equivalent of forty-two to fifty stocks in ten hours, as against one stock in the same length of time under former conditions. In this particular calling, then, there is a displacement of forty-four to forty-nine men in one operation.

Looking at a cruder industry, that of brickmaking, improved devices have displaced ten per cent of labor, while in making fire-brick forty per cent of the labor formerly employed is now dispensed with, and yet in many brickmaking concerns no displacement whatever has taken place.

The manufacture of boots and shoes offers some very wonderful facts in this connection. In one large and long-established manufactory in one of the Eastern States the proprietors testify that it would require five hundred persons, working by hand processes and in the old way in the shops by the roadside, to make as many women's boots and shoes as one hundred persons now make with the aid of machinery and by congregated labor, a contraction of eighty per cent in this particular case. In another division of the same industry the number of men required to produce a given quantity of boots and shoes has been reduced one half, while, in still another locality, and on another quality of boots, being entirely for women's wear, where formerly a first-class workman could turn out six pairs in one week, he will now turn out eighteen pairs. A well-known firm in the West engaged in the manufacture of boots and shoes finds that it would take one hundred and twenty persons, working by hand, to produce the amount of work done in its factory by sixty employees, and that the handwork would not compare in workmanship and appearance by fifty per cent. By the use of Goodyear's sewing machine for turned shoes one man will sew two hundred and fifty pairs in one day. It would require eight men, working by hand, to sew the same number in the same time. By the use of a heel-shaver or trimmer one man will trim three hundred pairs of shoes a day, while formerly three men would have been required to do the same work; and with the McKay machine one operator will handle three hundred pairs of shoes in one day, while without the machine he could handle but five pairs in the same time. So, in nailing on heels, one man, with the aid of machinery, can heel three hundred pairs of shoes per day, while five men would have to work all day to accomplish this by hand. A large Philadelphia house which makes boys' and children's shoes entirely, has learned that the introduction of new machinery within the past thirty years has displaced employees in the proportion of six to one, and that the cost of the product has been reduced one half. . . .

In another line labor has been displaced to such an extent that only one third the number of operatives formerly required is now in employment. In the days of the single-spindle hand-wheel, one spinner, working fifty-six hours continuously, could spin five hanks of number thirty-two twist. At the present time, with one pair of self-acting mule-spinning machines, having 2,124 spindles, one spinner, with the assistance of two small boys, can produce

55,098 hanks of number thirty-two twist in the same time. It is quite generally agreed that there has been a displacement, taking all processes of cotton manufacture into consideration, in the proportion of three to one. The average number of spindles per operative in the cotton-mills of this country in 1831 was 25.2; it is now over 64.82, an increase of nearly 157 per cent; and along with this increase of the number of spindles per operative there has been an increase of product per operative of over 145 per cent, so far as spinning alone is concerned. In weaving in the olden time, in this country, a fair adult hand-loom weaver wove from forty-two to forty-eight yards of common shirting per week. Now a weaver, tending six power-looms in a cotton factory, will produce 1,500 yards and over in a single week; and now a recent invention will enable a weaver to double this product. . . .

And so illustrations might be accumulated in very many directions—in the manufacture of furniture, in the glass industry, in leather-making, in sawing lumber, in the manufacture of machines and machinery, in the production of metals and metallic goods of all kinds, or of wooden-ware, in the manufacture of musical instruments, in mining, in the oil industry, in the manufacture of paper, in pottery, in the production of railroad supplies, in the manufacture of rubber boots, of saws, of silk goods, of soap, of tobacco, of trunks, in building vessels, in making wine, and in the production of woolen goods.

It is impossible to arrive at an accurate statement as to the number of persons it would require under the old system to produce the goods made by the present industrial system with the aid of invention and power machinery. Any computation would be a rough estimate. In some branches of work such a rough estimate would indicate that each employee at the present represents, on an average, fifty employees under the old system. In many other branches the estimate would involve the employment of one now where three were employed. Looking at this question without any desire to be mathematically accurate, it is fair to say, perhaps, that it would require from fifty to one hundred million persons in this country, working under the old system, to produce the goods made and do the work performed by the workers of to-day with the aid of machinery. This computation may, of course, be very wide of the truth, but any computation is equally startling, and when it is considered that in spinning alone 1,100 threads are easily spun now at one time where one was spun under the old system, no estimate can be successfully disputed.

All these facts and illustrations simply show that there has been, economically speaking, a great displacement of labor by the use of inventions; power machinery has come in as a magical assistant to the power of muscle and mind, and it is this side of the question that usually causes alarm. Enlightenment has taught the wage-receiver some of the advantages of the introduction of inventions as his assistants, but he is not yet fully instructed as to their influence in all directions. He does see the displacement; he does see the difficulty of turning his hand to other employment or of finding employment in the same direction. These are tangible influences which present themselves squarely in the face of the man involved, and to him no philosophical, economic, or ethical answer is sufficient. It is therefore impossible to treat of the influence of inventions, so far as the displacement of labor is concerned, as one of the leading influences, on the individual basis. We must take labor abstractly. So, having shown the powerful influence of the use of ingenious devices in the displacement or contraction of labor, as such, it is proper to show how such devices have influenced the expansion of labor or created employments and opportunities for employment which did not exist before their inception and application. A separate chapter is given to this part of the subject.

CHAPTER XXVIII: THE INFLUENCE OF MACHINERY ON LABOR.—EXPANSION

As incredible as the facts given in the preceding chapter appear to one who has not studied them, the ability to crystallize in individual cases and show the fairly exact displacement of labor exists. An examination of the opposite influence of inventions, that of the expansion or creation of employments not before existing, reveals a more encouraging state or condition of things, but one in which the statistician can make but very little headway. The influences under the expansion of labor have various ramifications. The people at large, and especially those who work for wages, have experienced these influences in several directions, and contemporaneous with the introduction and use of inventions, the chief economic influence being in the direction of expansion, the other influences being more thoroughly ethical, and these should be considered under that broad title. The statistical method helps in some respects in studying the expansive power of inventions, and especially in the direction of great staples used as raw material in manufacturing processes and in the increase of the number of people employed relative to the number of the population. If there has been a great increase in the consumption per capita of great staples for manufacturing purposes, there must have been a corresponding expansion of labor necessary for the production of goods in like directions.

Taking up some of the leading staples, the facts show that the per capita consumption of cotton in this country in 1830 was 5.9 pounds; in 1880, 13.91 pounds; while in 1890 the per capita consumption had increased to nearly 19 pounds. These figures are for cotton consumed in our own country, and clearly and positively indicate that the labor necessary for such consumption has been kept up to the standard, if not beyond the standard, of the olden time —that is, as to the number of people employed.

In iron the increase has been as great proportionately. In 1870 the per capita consumption of iron in the United States was 105.64 pounds, in 1880 it had risen to 204.99, and in 1890 to 283.38. While processes in manufacturing iron have been improved, and labor displaced to a certain extent by such processes, this great increase in the consumption of iron is a most encouraging fact, and proves that there has been an offset to the displacement.

The consumption of steel shows like results. In 1880 it was 46 pounds per capita, and in 1890, 144 pounds. The application of iron and steel in all directions, in the building trades as well as in the mechanic arts, in great engineering undertakings, and in a multitude of directions, only indicates that labor must be actively employed, or such extensions could not take place. But a more conclusive offset to the displacement of labor, considered abstractly, is shown by the statistics of persons engaged in all occupations. From 1860 to 1890, a period of thirty years, and the most prolific period in this country of inventions, and therefore of the most intensified influence in all directions of their introduction, the population increased 99.16 per cent, while during the same period the number of persons employed in all occupations—manufacturing, agriculture, domestic service, everything—increased 176.07 per cent. In the twenty years, 1870 to 1890, the population increased 62.41 per cent, while the number of persons in all occupations increased 81.80 per cent. An analysis of these statements shows that the increase of the number of those engaged in manufacturing, mechanical, and mining industries, those in which the influence of inventions is most keenly felt, for the period from 1860 to 1890 was 172.27 per cent, as against 99.16 per cent increase in the total population. If statistics could be as forcibly applied to show the new occupations brought into existence by invention, it is believed that the result would be still more emphatic.

If we could examine scientifically the number of created occupations, the claim that inventions have displaced labor on the whole would be conclusively and emphatically refuted. Taking some of the great industries that now exist, and which did not exist prior to the inventions which made them, we must acknowledge the power of the answer. In telegraphy thousands and thousands of people are employed where no one has ever been displaced. The construction of the lines, the manufacture of the instruments, the operation of the lines—all these divisions and subdivisions of a great industry have brought thousands of intelligent men and women into remunerative employment where no one had ever been employed before. The telephone has only added to this accumulation and expansion, and the whole field of electricity, in providing for the employment of many skilled workers, has not trenched upon the privileges of the past. Electroplating, a modern device, has not only added wonderfully to the employed list by its direct influence, but indirectly by the introduction of a class of goods which can be secured by all persons. Silverware is no longer the luxury of the rich. Through the invention of electroplating, excellent ware, with most artistic design, can be found in almost every habitation in America. The application of electroplating to nickel furnished a subsidiary industry to that of electroplating generally, and nickelplating had not been known half a dozen years before more than thirty thousand people were employed in the industry, where no one had ever been employed prior to the invention. . . .

It is certainly true—and the statement is simply cumulative evidence of the truth of the view that expansion of labor through inventions has been equal or superior to any displacement that has taken place—that in those countries given to the development and use of machinery there is found the greatest proportion of employed persons, and that in those countries where machinery has been developed to little or no purpose poverty reigns, ignorance is the prevailing condition, and civilization consequently far in the rear.

The expansion of values as the result of the influence of machinery has been quite as marvelous as in any other direction, for educated labor, supplemented by machinery, has developed small quantities of inexpensive material into products of great value. This truth is illustrated by taking cotton and iron ore as the starting-point. A pound of cotton, costing at the time this calculation was made but 13 cents, has been developed into muslin which sold in the market for 80 cents, and into chintz which sold for $4. Seventy-five cents' worth of common iron ore has been developed into $5 worth of bar-iron, or into $10 worth of horse-shoes, or into $180 worth of table knives, or into $6,800 worth of fine needles, or into $29,480 worth of shirt buttons, or into $200,000 worth of watch-springs, or $400,000 worth of hair-springs, and the same quantity of common iron ore can be made into $2,500,000 worth of pallet arbors.

The illustrations given, both of the expansion of labor and the expansion of values, are sufficiently suggestive of a line of study which, carried in any direction, will show that machinery is the friend and not the enemy of man, especially when man is considered as a part of society and not as an individual.

VAN NOSTRAND ANVIL BOOKS already published